OXFORD E

TOURISM ①

Robin Walker and Keith Harding

Student's Book

Audio-CD: EG 36855

OXFORD
UNIVERSITY PRESS

Contents

1 What is tourism?

Take off

pilot	waiter
tour guide	resort rep
flight attendant	chef
tourist information officer	porter
travel agent	hotel manager
receptionist	airline check-in clerk

1 What jobs do the people in the pictures do? Choose from the list.

2 Put the other jobs into categories, for example, *travel jobs*, *hotel jobs*.

3 How many different categories are there? Can you think of other tourism jobs for each of the categories? If you don't know the name, describe or mime what the person does.

4 What is the best job in tourism in your opinion?

Tourism: the world's biggest industry ... the world's best jobs

Vocabulary

Adjectives for job skills

With a partner, look at the adjectives for describing people.

1 Find six pairs of opposite adjectives.

calm	friendly	flexible	extrovert
nervous	lazy	smart	shy
disorganized	creative	confident	hardworking
scruffy	practical	organized	unfriendly

2 Choose one of the jobs in *Take off*. Say which three qualities are the most important.

Speaking

Careers questionnaire

1 What is your working style? Look at the questionnaire and tick (✓) the qualities and skills which describe you.

Questionnaire

QUALITIES

I am

smart	☐	extrovert	☐	hardworking	☐
flexible	☐	organized	☐	practical	☐
creative	☐	friendly	☐	confident	☐

SKILLS

I enjoy meeting new people.	☐
I enjoy working as part of a team.	☐
I like working independently.	☐
I am good at explaining things.	☐
I am good at dealing with people.	☐
I can make people relax.	☐
I am able to do more than one thing at the same time.	☐
I like working under pressure.	☐
I know how to use computers and technology.	☐
I feel confident about dealing with money.	☐
I am willing to work long hours.	☐
I am good at languages.	☐

2 Discuss your answers with a partner.

3 Which three skills are most important for a career in tourism?

Language spot

Describing job skills

Look at the sentences for describing job skills and abilities.

+ infinitive	+ *-ing* or noun
I can make people relax.	I enjoy meeting new people.
I know how to use computers.	I like working independently.
I am willing to work long hours.	I am good at languages.
I am able to do more than one thing at the same time.	I feel confident about dealing with money.

1 Complete the paragraph. Choose from the words in the list.

be / being	understand / understanding
smile / smiling	use / using
speak / speaking	work / working

So you want to work in tourism?

What do you have to do? What do you need to know?

In most tourism jobs you have to enjoy _____¹ with people – not just the customers but your colleagues as well. You have to be able to _____² as part of a team. You have to know how to _____³, even if you're having a bad day. It's also important to be able to _____⁴ clearly on the phone. In many jobs you need to be good at _____⁵ people with different languages and cultures, and you need to be confident about _____⁶ the languages that you know. Sometimes, especially if you work in an office, you have to know how to _____⁷ computers. It's also important to be flexible, and you often have to be willing to _____⁸ long or unusual hours. But most of all you have to like _____⁹ with people.

2 Look back at the jobs in *Take off*. What skills and abilities do you think they need?

EXAMPLE

A flight attendant has to be willing to work long hours.

>> Go to **Grammar reference** p.119

Andrew Sharpe

Personal details
Age 28
Single
Born in the Parish of Manchester, Jamaica

Tourism experience

Started in tourism at the age of twelve, as an assistant in a restaurant

Trained on the Cayman Islands – one-year work experience as a chef

Other tourism jobs: hotel front desk, car rental supervisor, night manager of a small hotel, check-in clerk for a charter airline

Present job

Runs his own tour company ('Authentic Caribbean Holidays Ltd.')

Promotes 'Unique Jamaica' programme (adventure travel)

Attends trade fairs

Runs in-school programmes for Jamaican students to teach tourism development, sustainability, and community tourism

Offers internships and work experience for university students

'There's so much to do in tourism. There are many aspects: hotels, water sports, tour operation, travel agents.'

What do you need to succeed in tourism?

'Working in tourism is about love – love for the industry. If you don't love it, forget it. It's a people industry. It's providing service. It's people enjoying and experiencing your culture. That's crucial. If you don't have that love, it doesn't make sense. If you work in the industry, you've got to love it.'

It's my job

Read about Andrew Sharpe from Jamaica.

1 When did Andrew start working in tourism?

2 What jobs has he done in tourism?

3 What does he do now?

4 What does he think is important when you work in tourism?

5 What does he want to do in the future?

What do you like about tourism?

'You get to experience different cultures, coming to Europe to see how they operate and live, what they like … In Europe you see something done differently which can help you with the same procedure back home, looking at it from a different angle. Even travelling inter-island, visiting various islands, then you see "OK, this island does it this way, we do it that way", and so forth.'

What do you do to relax?

'As a Caribbean, part of our life is enjoyment – having fun, our music, food, culture – it's natural for us. I play cricket. I love cricket, with friends, on the beach, and football …'

What's the future for you?

'My goal is hopefully to become Minister of Tourism, Director of Tourism, that's my main goal. You have to have a rounded knowledge of the industry, from ground level to the top.'

Listening
Three jobs

1 Kelly   2 John   3 Suzanna

1 🎧 Listen to three people talking about their jobs.

  1 Which job do they each have? Choose from the list in *Take off*.

  2 Which of them

    a enjoys working with people?
    b gets one day off a week?
    c works shifts?
    d works mainly in the back office?
    e only works part of the year?

2 🎧 Listen again and complete the extracts.

Extract 1

I _____¹ arrivals, hand out _____², process enquiries and _____³, that kind of thing. I work _____⁴, which can be a drag. I _____⁵ start at six in the morning, which is OK because I get off nice and early, but then _____⁶ I do the late turn and I don't finish till after midnight – this week I _____⁷ the late shift.

Extract 2

I _____⁸ directly with the public at the desk. On a typical day, I'm on the phone and the _____⁹ most of the time. I _____¹⁰ the day by checking my _____¹¹, and that _____¹² the agenda for the first part of the morning at least. I have to talk to local businesses, hotels, tour companies, to check that _____¹³ the service they want, that we're stocking their brochures and so on. I also _____¹⁴ presentations, and I get invited to a lot of social events to network and talk about tourism information services in the city.

I _____¹⁵ on a big presentation for some Italian clients at the moment.

Extract 3

We work very _____¹⁶, especially on changeover days. We take the _____¹⁷ who are going home to the airport at six in the morning, and bring back the new group. We then have to get them settled, sort out any _____¹⁸ – and there always are problems! – and do the paperwork. So I _____¹⁹ until midnight on changeover day.

● Language spot
Describing job routines

EXAMPLE

*Kelly: 'I usually **start** at six in the morning ... but this week I**'m doing** the late shift.'*

1 Which of the verbs describes a habitual action and which describes a temporary activity or arrangement?

2 Underline other examples of the tenses in *Listening* **2**.

3 Complete these sentences with the correct form of the verb in brackets.

  1 I usually _____ (finish) at five, but today I _____ (work) until eight.

  2 We _____ (not have) many guests outside the summer season, but a big conference _____ (take place) this weekend, so we're very busy.

  3 Some of the rooms _____ (not have) private bathrooms. Which room _____ (stay) in, madam?

  4 I _____ (wait) for a call from the manager. She _____ (want) me to show some important clients our deluxe suites. They _____ (think) of holding a business meeting there.

  5 I _____ (work) with computers a lot. In fact, I _____ (do) a special training course at the moment. I _____ (go) to college every Tuesday evening.

» Go to **Grammar reference** p.119

What is tourism?
Tourism is the temporary short-term movement of people to destinations outside the places where they normally live and work, and their activities during the stay at these destinations.
Tourism Society
UK, 1991

This is the stuff that changed the world. Along with a handful of other things – television, sex, and the computer – the ability to travel the world freely sets those who live in the late 20th century (and early 21st century) apart from those who lived before it.
Michael Elliot
1991, 'The Pleasure Principle'. The Economist, London

Speaking
Job skills

1 What questions would you ask to find out this information about the two people?

Nationality	*Where does he / she come from?*
Age	
Job	
Qualities and skills	
Working hours	
Typical daily tasks	
Things he / she enjoys about the job	
Relaxing after work	
Own holidays	

2 Work in pairs. Student A, look at p. 108. Student B, look at p. 118. Ask about each other's person.

Vocabulary
Industry sectors

1 The travel and tourism industry has different sectors. Look at the diagram and match the descriptions a – f below with the six sectors.

a   people or companies that organize and assemble the different parts of a holiday or tour

b   places to stay, such as hotels, and the food and services that are provided there

c   places that tourists want to visit

d   ways of travelling between different places, such as trains and airplanes

e   government organizations that promote and develop tourism

f   people or companies that sell the holiday or tour to the customer

Pronunciation

1 🎧 Listen to these words. How many syllables do they have? Tick (✓) the right column.

	Number of syllables			Strongest
Word	1	2	3	
agent		✓		*first*
attendant				
manager				
catering				
guide				–
porter				
tourism				
pilot				
attractions				
calm				–

2 🎧 Listen to the words with two or three syllables. Which syllable is strongest?

3 Say each word. Let your partner check your pronunciation.

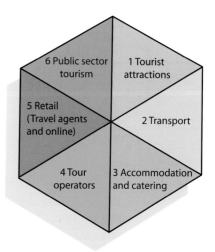

2 Think of a local example for each of the sectors from your city or country, for example, the name of a local travel agent.

tourism /ˈtʊərɪzəm/ NOUN [U] the business of providing and arranging holidays and services for people who are visiting a place

Customer care

'The customer is always right'

1 Do you agree that 'the customer is always right'?

2 Look at this definition. Think of your own good experiences as a customer. Tell your partner about them.

> **Tourism is about customer care:**
> It's about people, not just places.
> It's about always smiling.
> It's about always listening.
> It's about delighting the customer, not just serving the customer.
> It's about loving your job, not just doing it.

Find out

1 Where can you find out facts and statistics on tourism in your country?

2 What are the names of the main tourism companies in your country? Find their websites and note down information on what they do, when they were founded, what jobs they provide – and anything else that you find interesting.

Writing

Country fact sheet

Complete this fact sheet for your country (or region).

FACT SHEET

Name of country / region: ....

Sources for information and statistics: ....

	Website	Location
National tourism board (or office)	....	....
Regional / local tourism office (TIC)	....	....
Other useful websites	....	....

Sector	Example company	Website	Location	Other information (e.g. size, no. of visitors, branches, etc.)
Tourism attractions				
Transport				
Accommodation and catering				
Tour operators				
Travel agents				

challenge (n) something new and difficult that forces you to make a lot of effort

currency (n) the system and type of money that a particular country uses

economy (n) the operation of a country's money supply, commercial activities, and industry

flexible (adj) that can be changed easily

security (n) the state of feeling safe and being free from worry

Reading

Tourism: the biggest business in the world

1 Discuss these statements with a partner. Write T (true) or F (false).

  1 One in fifty of all workers are employed in tourism related industries.

  2 The number of international tourism arrivals will more than double between 2004 and 2020.

  3 Tourists often worry about international security.

  4 Tourism has only had a good influence on the modern world.

2 Read the article to check your answers.

TOURISM TODAY

Facts and challenges

Tourism is one of the biggest businesses in the world. There are nearly 800 million international tourist arrivals every year. It employs, directly or indirectly, one in fifteen of all workers worldwide, from A to Z, from airport cleaners to zookeepers, and includes bar staff, flight attendants, tour guides, and resort reps. It is a huge part of the **economy** of many countries – in countries such as the Bahamas, over 60% of the economy is based on tourism.

Tourism is a fast-growing business. When Thomas Cook organized his first excursion from Leicester to Loughborough in 1841, he probably didn't know what he was starting. Key developments in the last 150 years or so have led to the rise of mass tourism. There have been technological developments in transport, in particular the appearance of air travel and charter flights. There have been changes in working practices, with workers getting paid holiday time and working shorter and more **flexible** hours.

In recent years we have seen the growth of the Internet and globalization, making the world seem a smaller but very fascinating place. The tourism industry grows faster and faster each year. In 1950, there were 25 million international tourist arrivals. In 2004, the figure was 760 million, and by 2020 it is predicted to be 1.6 billion.

But what are the **challenges** today? The tourism industry is affected by many different things: international events, economic change, changes in fashion. New concerns and worries appear every year, for example as people become more worried about **security** and international terrorism, or as the value of their **currency** changes. But new destinations and new sources of tourists also seem to emerge every year.

Tourism survives. It is a powerful and sometimes dangerous force in the modern world. Tourism creates many good jobs and careers, but it also produces many poor and badly paid jobs. Tourism can help to protect environments and animal life, but it can also damage them. Tourism can save cultures and the local way of life, but it can also destroy them. Tourism can change countries – and people – for the better, but it can also change them for the worse.

Tourism is one of the biggest industries in the world. It is perhaps also the most important

3 In pairs, answer and discuss these questions.

1 What do these numbers in paragraphs 2 and 3 refer to?
   a 1841
   b 25 million
   c 760 million
   d 1.6 billion

2 What are the four positive and four negative effects of tourism mentioned in the article?

3 How many jobs in tourism can you think of?

   EXAMPLES
   A is for airline check-in clerk.
   B is for baggage handler.
   C is for…

4 Which of the key developments in tourism do you think were the most important?

5 Can you think of some recent international events that have affected the tourism industry?

6 Do you think tourism is a positive or a negative influence in the world?

Vocabulary

Personal Learning Dictionaries (PLD)

1 Look back at the dictionary entry for the word *tourism* on p. 9. How many different pieces of information does the dictionary give you?

2 Which of the pieces of information in this list is not in the dictionary?
   ● The word (e.g. *tourism*)
   ● Its translation in your language
   ● The phonetic transcription (e.g. /ˈtʊərɪzəm/)
   ● The part of speech (e.g. *noun*)
   ● Any relevant grammar or language features (e.g. *uncountable*)
   ● Use in an example sentence (e.g. *Tourism is the world's biggest industry and employs millions of people throughout the world.*)
   ● Related words (e.g. *tourist*)
   ● Any other important information

3 Select the most important words from this unit. For each word, prepare an entry for your Personal Learning Dictionary.

Checklist

Assess your progress in this unit. Tick (✓) the statements which are true.

   I can understand articles describing the tourism industry

   I can understand people talking about their jobs in tourism

   I can describe job / work routines and skills

   I can ask questions about the personal profiles of tourism employees

Key words

Jobs
check-in clerk
chef
flight attendant
pilot
porter
receptionist
resort rep
tour guide
tourist information officer
tour operator
travel agent
waiter

Nouns
catering
charter flight
destination
excursion
public sector
retail
shift
tourist attraction

Adjectives
online
worldwide

Next stop

1 Which countries have you visited as a tourist? Which countries would you like to visit? Why?

2 What famous attractions have you seen?

3 Which was your favourite, and why?

2 World destinations

Take off

1 Do you know the names of these famous attractions?

2 Match them with the outline map of the country where they are located. What are the names of the countries?

3 What type of attraction is each one? Choose from the list.

historic monument   beach
theme park   cathedral
castle   temple
natural geographic feature   ski resort
palace

4 Can you find these types of attractions in your country? Give examples.

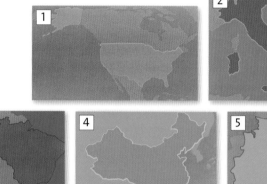

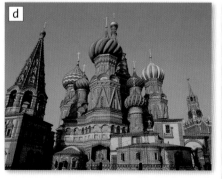

Pronunciation

Look at the dictionary transcriptions of some countries and cities.

speɪn	ˈrʌʃə	məˈdrɪd
frɑːns	ˈkænədə	ˈpærɪs
ˈlʌndən	ˈɪtəli	ˈhʌŋɡəri
ˈmeksɪkəʊ	ˈmɒskəʊ	ˈtəʊkijəʊ
ˈtʃaɪnə	ˈæθənz	ˈdʒɜːməni
rəʊm	dʒəˈpæn	brəˈzɪl

1 Can you find the following places?

1 Spain
2 France
3 Japan
4 China
5 Russia

2 Identify the other places.

3 🎧 Listen and identify the ten places you hear.

4 🎧 Listen again and repeat each place.

5 Practise saying the place names from the dictionary transcription.

6 How do you know where the stress is in words with more than one syllable?

Listening

Where do tourists go?

1 When we look at the movement of tourists (or *tourist flow*), there are three types of tourism. Match the words below with their definitions.

1 domestic tourism
2 inbound tourism
3 outbound tourism

a people leaving their country to take holidays
b people taking holidays in their own country
c people entering the country from abroad to take holidays

2 Which countries do you think receive the greatest number of tourists?

3 🎧 Listen to the numbers. Which one do you hear?
a 19,000 / 90,000   c 13.5 / 30.5
b 18 million / 80 million   d 15 / 50

4 🎧 Listen and repeat the numbers.

19   90   18   80   13   30   15   50

5 Write down some similar numbers. Do not show them to your partner. Read them to each other. Can you identify them correctly?

6 🎧 Listen to this presentation describing the top ten country destinations for tourists. Complete the table.

Position	Country	Number of tourists
1st		
2nd		
3rd		
4th		
5th		
6th		
7th		
8th		
9th		
10th		

7 What do you know about the ten countries as tourist destinations? Think about the following categories and give examples.

- Towns and cities
- Natural attractions and features (e.g. beaches)
- Historical and cultural attractions
- Purpose-built attractions (e.g. theme parks)

8 Think about your own country.

1 Where do domestic tourists go? What attractions do they visit?

2 What places do inbound tourists visit? Which countries do they come from?

3 Where do outbound tourists go? Which countries do they visit?

80% of all international travel is made up of nationals of just twenty countries.

In 2004, an estimated 760m tourists travelled internationally, or nearly 12% of the world's people.

In Hawaii, American and Japanese tourists outnumber Hawaiians by five to one in the summer.

Reading

Where do tourists come from?

1 Which countries do you think generate the most tourists?

2 Look at this graph of the eleven highest tourist-generating countries. Can you identify each country from the first letter and flag?

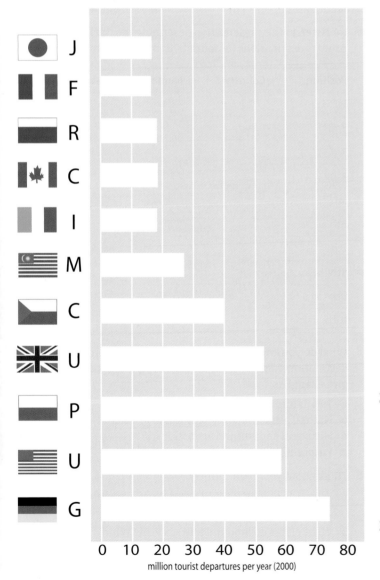

million tourist departures per year (2000)

3 Does any of the information surprise you?

Speaking

The biggest spenders and the biggest earners

1 Look at the word grid and complete the sentences.

earn (v) to get money by working

receive (v) to get or accept sth that sb sends or gives to you

spend (v) to give or pay money for sth

Verb	spend	earn	receive
Noun (person)	spender	earner	-
Noun (thing)	expenses expenditure	earnings	receipt

1 If you _____ more than you _____ , you will get into debt. But if you _____ more than you _____ , you can save.

2 The IT manager is one of the highest _____ in the company. His total _____ are twice what I _____ .

3 When you are on a business trip you can claim things like travel and hotel costs as _____ . But you must remember to get a _____ .

4 The travel agency didn't make a profit last year because the _____ was greater than the _____ from customers.

2 Which of these countries do you think are the biggest tourist spenders, and which are the biggest tourist earners?

Austria	Germany	the Netherlands
Canada	Greece	the UK
China	Italy	the USA
France	Japan	

3 Work in pairs. Student A, look at p.108. Student B, look at p.113. Give your information to your partner and complete the blank chart.

4 Compare your charts. Identify the countries which receive more from tourism than they spend.

Vocabulary

Tourism features and attractions

The things that attract tourists to a particular country can be divided into different groups. Look at the table.

Climate	Natural features	Built attractions	Events	Food, drink, and entertainment	Accommodation	Transport
rainy	beach	cathedral	carnival	restaurant	hotel	train
sunny	desert	museum	folk dance	bar	motel	plane

1 Decide which column the words in the list should go in (there may be more than one possibility). You can use an English–English dictionary.

harbour	castle	damp
music festival	concert	metro
campsite	countryside	nightlife
waterfall	art gallery	temperate
chilly	heritage	coastline

2 Complete the sentences.

1 I don't really like the city. I prefer to live in the
_____ .

2 There aren't many beaches on the island. The
_____ is mainly rocky with steep cliffs.

3 The Netherlands has a _____ climate, with
mild winters and cool summers.

4 These beautiful old churches are part of our national
_____ .

3 Can you think of any other words to add to the table?

4 Work with a partner. Use the new words to talk about
your region or your favourite holiday destination.

Customer care

Different destinations – different customs

Working in tourism means meeting people from
different countries. It also means sending people to
different destinations with different traditions and
customs. It is important to respect and understand
these different traditions and customs.

1 How can you find out more about the traditions of
visitors from some of the countries listed in this unit?

2 How can you help tourists to understand local traditions
and cultures when they visit other destinations?

Where in the world?

1 What do you know about New Zealand and the Balearic Islands? Think about: climate, geography and location, natural features, main attractions, and their importance as a tourist destination.

2 Now read the descriptions and check your answers.

3 Which text would you find
1 in a reference book?
2 in an advertisement or brochure?

The Balearic Islands – Majorca, Minorca, Ibiza, Formentera

New Zealand

Capital: Wellington
Population: 4 million
Currency: New Zealand dollar
Official languages: English and Maori

New Zealand lies in the South Pacific Ocean and consists of two islands – North Island and South Island. It is located 1,600 km south-east of Australia and is nearly 2,000 km long.

The climate is generally temperate and damp, although the extreme north has got an almost subtropical climate and the extreme south is very cold. Winds can be a problem: the capital (Wellington) is known for its high winds.

The main attraction for tourists is the scenery. The landscape is largely unspoilt and very varied. There are mountains, lakes, glaciers, rainforests, dramatic coastlines, beaches, and geysers.

Other attractions include the Maori culture and outdoor activities such as river-rafting, fishing, skiing, whale-watching, and bungee-jumping (which was a local invention).

Tourists come mainly from Australia, the United States, the United Kingdom, and Japan. Tourism is the largest single foreign exchange earner and continues to grow. An increase in visitor numbers followed the huge success of the *Lord of the Rings* films, which were made in New Zealand.

* **Sun, sea, and culture – with a Spanish style**
* **300 days a year of guaranteed sunshine**
* **Fabulous beaches**
* **Easy to get to**
* **Great entertainment**
* **Something for every type of tourist**

Floating between Spain and the North African coast, the Balearic Islands offer the perfect location for a fantastic holiday. There are four main islands for you to choose from, each with their own special atmosphere.

The gorgeous climate boasts more than 300 days a year of guaranteed sunshine, making the islands the ideal setting for a beach holiday. The long hot summer stretches from May to October, with temperatures around 27°C – just right for relaxing and getting a tan.

The islands offer a number of attractions for tourists. Sun-seekers will love the fabulous beaches. Fun-seekers will enjoy the exciting nightlife – the clubs and discos of Ibiza provide plenty of entertainment for young people. But there's more to these islands than sun and fun. You can also enjoy wonderful architecture (the Gothic cathedral at Palma is well worth visiting), hilltop villages, olive groves, great food, and hidden beaches. You can take a relaxing fishing or sailing trip, or go to one of the many festivals. If you go in June, don't miss the spectacular Fiesta of San Juan at Ciutadella on Minorca.

Whatever you want from a holiday, the Balearics will help you find it.

● Language spot

Describing resources and features

	New Zealand	The Balearic Islands
Describing geographical features	New Zealand **lies** in the South Pacific Ocean. **It consists of** two islands. **It is located** 1,600 km south-east of Australia.	
Describing climate	**The climate is generally** temperate and damp. **The extreme north has got** an almost subtropical climate.	
Describing tourist attractions	**The main attraction for tourists is** the scenery. **The landscape is** largely unspoilt and very varied. **There are** mountains, lakes, glaciers …	

1 Look at the expressions used to describe resources and features in the text on New Zealand.

Does the text on the Balearic Islands use the same expressions?

2 Which different expressions does it use to describe the three areas? The verbs listed below will help you identify them.

| float | choose | stretch | provide |
| offer | boast | love | enjoy |

3 The text on the Balearic Islands is trying to attract visitors. One way it does this is to use sentences where the subject is 'you'. Find the sentences using 'you'.

4 Use the sentences you identified in **2** and **3** to help you to write similar sentences for New Zealand.

EXAMPLE
Floating in the South Pacific Ocean, New Zealand offers the perfect location for an exciting holiday.

5 Use the sentences about New Zealand in the table to write similar sentences for the Balearic Islands.

EXAMPLE
The Balearic Islands lie between Spain and the North African coast.

» Go to **Grammar reference** p.120

Listening
Favourite places

2 What do they like about each of their favourite places?

3 🎧 Listen again to Liz. Match the four adjectives with the four nouns to form word combinations.

A	B
remote	views
spectacular	coastline
ruined	cottage
dramatic	castle

4 Match these eight adjectives and eight nouns to form more word combinations. Then check your answers with the listening script on p. 128.

A	B
cheap	memories
cultural	bars
delicious	beaches
happy	heritage
relaxing	nightlife
exciting	flights
lively	break
crowded	food

5 Work in pairs. Have you ever been to places with similar features, for example, *a dramatic coastline*? Tell each other about the places.

1 🎧 Listen to three people talking about their favourite holiday destinations.

Which of the places in the list do they each say is their favourite?

London	Budapest
Scotland	Prague
Northumberland	Barcelona
Zurich	Cyprus
Vienna	Ibiza

a Liz _____
b Regula _____
c Valery _____

Speaking

Describing a destination

1 Work in groups. Think of another destination (not your own country or region). Make statements to describe it to the other students in the group. Can they guess the place in less than ten statements? You get a point for every statement that doesn't lead to a successful guess.

2 What do you know about the Seychelles and South Africa?

Writing

Describing a destination

Write descriptions of two other tourist destinations, using the information files on p. 109. Make one a factual description, and the other more like an advertisement or brochure.

Find out

1 Think of a country or a region. It could be your own country or region or a country or region that you know well.

Where can you find out more about the place you have chosen as a tourist destination?

Find out as much as you can and record the information under the following headings.
- Location and geographic features
- Climate
- Transport
- Tourist attractions
- Other information

2 Use the information you have found out on the country or region to
- write a factual information sheet
- write a brochure description
- prepare a talk or presentation.

Use pictures and visuals where possible.

3 Present your talks in small groups. Listen to each other's talks, make notes, and ask questions.

Checklist

Assess your progress in this unit. Tick (✓) the statements which are true.

I can talk about tourist destinations and flows

I can understand and describe statistical charts and simple graphs

I can understand people talking about their favourite destinations

I can understand descriptions of resources and features in tourist destinations

I can produce descriptions of resources and features in tourist destinations

Key words

Specialist industry terms
domestic tourism
inbound tourism
outbound tourism
tourist flow

Nouns

carnival	harbour
cathedral	heritage
climate	historic monument
coastline	landscape
countryside	receipt
desert	temple
expenditure	theme park

Adjectives
remote
spectacular
temperate
unspoilt

Next stop

1 What different types of holiday have you had in the past?

2 What was your favourite holiday? Why?

3 How did you arrange the holiday – independently (by yourself), through a company, online, or some other way?

3 Tour operators

Take off

1 Look at the different package holidays. What type of holiday are they advertising?

2 Which holiday(s) would you choose? Why?

3 Have you or has anybody you know ever been on a package holiday?

4 Why do you think people go on package holidays? Think of three reasons. Compare your reasons with your partners.

> **package holiday** (US package tour) *noun* [C] a holiday that is organized by a company for a fixed price that includes the cost of travel, hotels, etc.

Listening

Why choose a package holiday?

1 Listen to Helga, who works for *Das Reise Büro*, a German tour operator. What are the reasons she gives for choosing a package holiday? Are they the same as yours?

2 Listen again and choose the correct answers.

1 How far in advance do tour operators buy accommodation or transport?

  a Six months
  b One year
  c Two years
  d Three years

2 What things does Helga say that people will need money for on a package holiday?

  a Buying drinks
  b Buying souvenirs
  c Car hire
  d Paying for taxis

3 According to Helga, what does a tour operator's representative, or 'rep', do?

4 Helga says that package holidays produce 'peace of mind'. What does she mean?

Reading

The role of tour operators

Read the article and find the answers.

1 Package holidays are created by tour operators and then sold through the *chain of distribution*.

   a What are the components of a typical package holiday?

   b Who else forms part of the *chain of distribution*?

   c How many different types of tour operator are there?

2 There are two other terms that mean the same as *package holiday*. What are they?

3 To *buy in bulk* means to buy something

   a on the Internet
   b in large quantities
   c in secret
   d a long time before you need to use it.

4 Why is it important to buy in bulk in tour operation?

5 Why do you think specialist tour operators prefer to sell direct to their clients?

6 If you could work for one of the four types of tour operator, which would you choose?

Putting a package together

Package holidays, which are also known as package tours, include all of the components necessary for a complete vacation:

- transport to and from the destination
- transfers between the airport / station / port and hotel
- food and accommodation at the destination
- other services such as a guide or holiday 'rep'.

The professionals who bring these elements together to create a holiday are called tour operators. They buy in advance and in bulk from the principals: airlines, shipping lines, hoteliers, and so on. Because they buy hundreds of seats or rooms from the principal, they pay a much lower price for them than an ordinary member of the public. The tour operator then converts this bulk into individual packages known technically as inclusive tours (ITs). These are marketed to the consumer through travel agents or by other systems.

In the past tour operators sold almost entirely through travel agents, but today they also use direct selling. This strategy eliminates the travel agents from the

chain of distribution, and this reduces the final cost of the holiday package because direct sell operators do not have to pay commission to a travel agent. Many smaller tour operators, for example, prefer to deal directly with their clients.

Not all tour operators sell the same type of holiday. The really big operators, the mass market operators, produce low-cost holidays to traditional sea, sun, and sand destinations like Spain, Greece, or Turkey. Other operators limit their

product to customers who want a very specific type of holiday. These specialist operators sell adventure holidays, holidays for single people, holidays for motor-racing fans, and so on. Domestic operators specialize in tours for people who want to holiday in their own country, whilst incoming tour operators are specialists in providing holiday packages to visitors coming from abroad. For example, 'Vastravel', an Italian incoming tour operator, sells tours of Italy to people from the rest of the world.

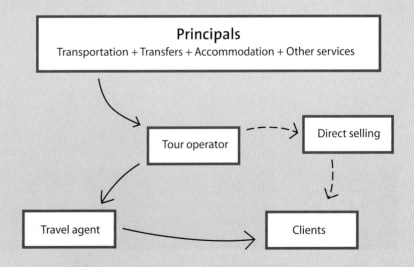

It's my job

Begoña Pozo

Fifteen years ago Begoña Pozo and her sister opened a travel agency because they both love to travel. Now she is the European agent for Myanmar Gold, a specialist tour operator for Burma. What do you think she likes about her job?

Now read on.

Begoña says:

… about her job I love to sell and to work in the office … to try to introduce the place to my clients, and to show them the place and tell them that they have to go there.

… about Burma Burma has started to attract tourists from all around the world. It's very beautiful and everything is so traditional.

… about Burmese people They're always smiling. And very often they give you presents because they are Buddhists. You can tell that religion is really important to them.

… about Asia I think that people in Europe are not as friendly as in Asia. Asian people are very friendly. On Thai Airways the flight attendants always bow when you enter the plane. On European airlines they often stand with their arms crossed. Asian culture is more polite.

Listening

The 'Peace in Burma' tour

Begoña's main job is organizing escorted tours of Burma, in south-east Asia.

1 Why do you think people visit Burma?

2 🎧 Listen to Begoña describing one of the tours she organizes. Tick (✓) the places the tour visits, and the activities the tourists can do.

Place	Activity
☐ Bagan	Rent a bicycle
☐ Bago	Spend some time at the beach
☐ Inle	Visit a school of Buddhism
☐ Mandalay	Go trekking in the mountains
☐ Ngapali	Practise yoga
☐ Sittwe	Visit the city's floating markets
☐ Thailand	Visit some of the many temples
☐ Thandwe	Go horse riding
☑ Yangon	Visit the capital city

3 🎧 Listen again. Which activities can you do in which place?

4 What is the main problem Begoña has when she tries to get people to go to Burma?

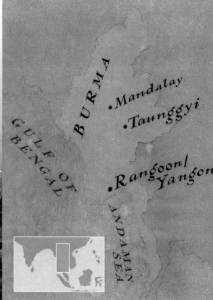

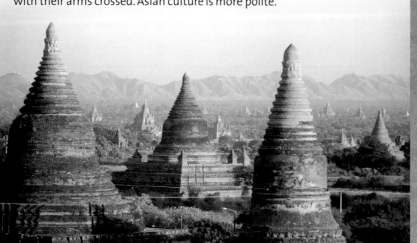

More than **12 million people** in the UK take a package holiday each year.

● Language spot

Asking questions

One-way tour operators like Begoña market their product is by attending tourism fairs. There they can meet other travel agents and direct-sell clients.

1 Look at the notes below. They were made by a travel agent who is looking for different types of package holiday to sell.

Brochures of tours?
Price include transfers?
Price include meals?
Use local hotels?
Accept groups?
Discount for groups?
How much?
Travel agent's commission – how much?

2 What were the questions the travel agent asked when talking to a tour operator?

EXAMPLES
Brochures of tours?
'Do you have brochures of your tours?'
Price include transfers?
'Does the price include transfers?'

3 Can you think of any other questions the travel agent might ask?

>> Go to **Grammar reference** p.120

Pronunciation

1 Say the following words. Pay attention to the stress. Is it on the first or second syllable?

accept   agent   local   travel

2 🎧 Listen to the words. Were you right?

3 🎧 Listen to the stress pattern in the following words and then write them in the right column in the table.

brochure	customer	holiday	package
commission	discount	include	providers
component	domestic	inclusive	transfers

●●	●●	●●●	●●●
agent	accept		
local			
travel			

4 Practise saying the words in each column.

Speaking

Talking to tour operators

1 Work in pairs. Student A, look at p.109 and study the information in the box. Student B, you are the travel agent. Look at p.114. Follow the instructions.

EXAMPLE
Tour operator *Good morning. Can I help you with anything?*
Travel agent *Yes, I hope so. I'm a travel agent from (your country / region). I'm looking for tours to …*

2 When you have finished, change roles and choose the information from a different tour operator.

former (adj) of an earlier time; belonging to the past

glimpse (n) a very quick and not complete view of sb / sth

Reading

An inclusive tour

Tour operators regularly use brochures and the Internet to advertise their package holidays and tours.

1 Look at the map of the Baltics. Read through the tour and connect the cities and other places in the order in which they are visited.

2 One of your clients is interested in visiting the Baltics. Look at the tour description and find the following information for the client.

1 The length of the tour

2 Departures for the second half of July or beginning of August

3 What type of accommodation will they have?

4 The basic price of the tour

5 How much will the tour cost for one person using a single room?

6 Does the cost of the tour include
   a all food and meals?
   b entry costs to monuments?
   c arrival and departure transfers?

7 Will there be a guide on the tour?

3 Work with a partner. Student A, you are the client. Student B, you are the travel agent. Ask and answer questions about the Baltics tour. When you have finished, change roles.

A **glimpse** of the **Baltics**

Vilnius – Riga – Tallinn
6 days by private coach

TOUR DESCRIPTION

Visit the three independent Baltic Republics of Estonia, Latvia, and Lithuania on this short escorted coach tour. The emphasis is on the capital cities.

FRIDAY **VILNIUS** Arrival. Transfer with private driver and guide. Check in at the hotel. At 7.00 p.m. welcome drink at the hotel where you will be greeted by tour guide or representative. Overnight at Hotel City Park or similar in Vilnius.

SATURDAY **VILNIUS – TRAKAI** Morning city tour of Vilnius, capital of Lithuania for more than 600 years. Afternoon trip to Trakai, **former** capital of Lithuania. Visit to a 14th century castle. For ages it served as a defensive structure and residence of Lithuanian Grand Dukes. Overnight at Hotel City Park.

SUNDAY **VILNIUS – RIGA** Morning departure by coach to Riga, the capital of Latvia. Visit to Rundale, a beautiful baroque palace south of Riga. It is a splendid example of the work of Italian architect F.B.Rastrelli. Arrival in Riga. Check in at the hotel. Overnight at Hotel Radisson SAS Daugava or similar in Riga.

Guaranteed departures: Fridays 20–
   Jun 8, 15, 22, 29
   Jul 6, 13, 20, 27
   Aug 3, 10, 17, 24

From: $845 per person double
   $345 single supplement

Includes:
◆ 5 nights at first-class hotels
◆ daily breakfast
◆ 1 welcome drink
◆ transportation by air-conditioned coach
◆ private arrival transfer
◆ sightseeing per itinerary
◆ local tour guides
◆ tax and service charges
◆ individual information package (city guides and programmes)

Riga

dawn (n) the early morning, when light first appears in the sky

navigable (adj) that boats can sail along

sacred (adj) connected with God, a god, or religion

snack (n) food that you can eat quickly between main meals

MONDAY RIGA – TALLINN In the morning a city tour of Riga, visiting the medieval town, Riga Castle, St. Peter's Church, the Old Guild Houses. Afternoon departure for Tallinn with a stop in Pärnu. Arrival in Tallinn. Check in at the hotel. Overnight at Hotel Domina Ilmarine or similar in Tallinn.

TUESDAY TALLINN Morning city tour of Tallinn, visiting the Old Town of Tallinn – an example of Gothic architecture in the Baltic and Nordic countries. The tour includes the Toompea Castle, the Russian Orthodox Cathedral, and the Town Hall Square. Afternoon free. Overnight at Domina Ilmarine or similar.

WEDNESDAY TALLINN DEPARTURE After breakfast, the tour ends with individual departures.

Vilnius

● **Language spot**

Prepositions of time

1 Match the prepositions *at, for, in*, and *on* with the time expressions on the right.

	Sunday
	Easter
	10 June
	the weekend
at	the afternoon
for	six days
in	night
on	the summer
	4 o'clock
	a long time
	2007

2 Use the correct preposition (*at, for, in, on*) to complete the itinerary.

> ### BASICALLY BOLIVIAN
>
> **Day 01** Arrive at La Paz International Airport. _____¹ 21.30h. Transfer to the hotel, check-in, and light supper.
>
> **Day 02** LA PAZ
>
> Half-day tour of La Paz. Try 'salteñas', a Bolivian **snack** that is only eaten _____² the morning. Afternoon free for shopping. Visit a traditional folk music 'peña' _____³ night.
>
> **Day 03** LA PAZ – LAKE TITICACA
>
> Leave after breakfast for the Tiwanaku ruins. _____⁴ more than 500 years Tiwanaku was the centre of American civilization.
>
> **Day 04** LAKE TITICACA
>
> Lake Titicaca, the **sacred** lake of the Incas, is the highest **navigable** lake in the world. We make an early start _____⁵ **dawn** to see the sun come up over the lake.

>> Go to **Grammar reference** p.121

Customer care

The personal touch

We always call our clients when they are on holiday in Burma so that we can make sure they are happy and change anything that they don't like.
Myanmar Gold representative

Coach tours can be very impersonal, so as the tour guide, I make a big effort to learn each person's name as soon as possible, and by the end of the second day of the tour at the latest.
Scantours representative

1 Have you ever experienced a holiday or a visit to a tourist attraction when you felt you received the *personal touch*?

2 How can tour operators give the *personal touch* to tourists before, during, and after their holiday or trip?

Speaking

Designing a package tour

1 You are going to prepare a five-day coach tour of your country or region. To do this, you will need to make decisions about
  1 which places you will visit
  2 which places you will overnight in
  3 how many nights you will spend in each place
  4 where your tour will begin and end
  5 which services and meals you will include in the price
  6 the different possible dates of your tour
  7 the name of your tour
  8 three ways you are going to personalize your tour.

2 Look at these phrases. They are often used by people in discussions.

Asking for suggestions
What can we call the tour?
Have you got any ideas about a name?

Making suggestions
We could call the tour…
Let's call the tour…
What about calling the tour… ?

Agreeing with a suggestion
Yes, OK.
Good idea.
That's fine by me.

Disagreeing with a suggestion
I don't know about that.
I don't think that's a very good idea.

3 Work in groups of three or four. Nominate one person to be the secretary. The secretary must write down the decisions about each point you discuss.

4 Plan your tour, and make sure that everybody participates in the discussion.

Writing

A web page for a package tour

Use the information from your discussion and write the text for a web page advertising your tour. You can use the web page for the Baltics Tour as a model.

Find out

1 Who are the biggest tour operators in your country or region?

2 Which are the most popular destinations they offer?

3 Which are the new destinations this year?

4 Do tour operators in your country only sell through travel agents or do they sell direct?

5 Are there any specialist tour operators in your country?

6 What type of specialist holidays do they market?

(Hint: for answers to these questions, look on the Internet or talk to a local travel agent.)

Writing

Describing local tour operations

Use the information you have collected by answering the questions in *Find out* and write a brief description of how tour operation works in your country.

You can begin like this:

Tour Operation in [the name of your country].

The biggest tour operators in [the name of your country / region] are [the names of two or three tour operators]. There are a number of important providers in our country, including [the names of any airlines, hotel groups, etc.] The most popular destinations that the tour operators offer every year are [the names of the usual destinations]. New offers this year include …

Checklist

Assess your progress in this unit. Tick (✓) the statements which are true.

    I can understand someone talking about package holidays

    I can understand articles about package tours and tour operation

    I can ask questions to get information about a package tour

    I can produce a tour itinerary for a web page or brochure

Key words

Nouns

brochure	package holiday / tour
client	provider
commission	representative ('rep')
direct selling	supplement
inclusive tour	tour operator
itinerary	transfer
operator	wholesaler

Adjectives
domestic
incoming
independent
specialist

Adverbs
in advance
in bulk

Verbs
include
overnight

Next stop

1 Do you have any friends or family who like going on holiday to places that are completely different from where they live?

2 What about you? When you go on holiday, do you like things that are completely new, or do you prefer things that are familiar?

4 Tourist motivations

Take off

1 Match the quotes with the pictures. Write quotes for the other two pictures.

2 Write down the last three trips you or members of your family made, and the reason.

EXAMPLE *Paris – weekend sightseeing trip*

3 Work in groups. Show each other the trips you wrote down. Can you put the different reasons into categories?

a
I like to be active on holiday – visit museums, galleries, that sort of thing.

b
We spent last Christmas in the mountains outside Kyoto – that's where my son lives now, his wife's Japanese.

c
I want to see as much of the world as possible. I'm meeting up with a bunch of friends next month and we're going hiking in the Himalayas.

d
We go to the beach every summer. I just want to relax and switch off and get some sun.

e
I have to visit our sales offices in Poland and the Netherlands four or five times a year. It's hard work, but I really like Poznań and Rotterdam.

In this unit
- motivation for travel
- describing purpose and reason
- describing trends
- changes in tourist motivation and behaviour

Reading

Why do people travel?

1 Read the text. How many of the types of trip you listed in *Take off* can you find?

2 Look again at the trips you listed and put them into the categories described in the text.

Inside tourism: reasons for travel

People travel for many different reasons. In the tourism industry we divide the reasons for travel into three main categories: leisure tourism, business tourism, and visiting friends and relatives (usually abbreviated to VFR).

Leisure tourism can mean anything from excursions, day trips, and weekend breaks to package holidays, pleasure cruises, and longer independent trips such as hillwalking or treks in the mountains. It also includes cultural trips (for example, to music festivals), educational trips (for example, study tours), and religious trips (for example, pilgrims on a walking tour to a holy place).

Business tourism includes any travel away from one's main place of residence, for such events as meetings, conferences, and trade fairs. It also includes special trips when workers are given a reward or a 'thank you' for good work (this is known as an incentive tour).

Travel in order to visit friends or family relatives is also regarded as part of the tourism industry. This could be for a special family party, such as a reunion or a wedding, or a regular trip made every year.

Listening

Reasons for travel and money spent on travel

The pie charts show the relative importance of the different categories of travel with reference to British tourists.

1 🎧 Listen to a lecture extract and label the percentages for each category.

a **Reasons for travel**

b **Money spent on travel**

- Leisure tourism
- Business tourism
- Visiting friends and relatives
- Other

2 Compare the two charts. Why do you think people travelling for leisure and for business spend more money than people travelling for VFR?

3 Use the information from the trips you listed in *Take off* to make a pie chart. How is it different from the chart for British tourists?

Vocabulary

Reasons for travel

1 Match the words in A with the definitions in B.

A		B
1	Sightseeing	a	A long hard walk lasting several days or weeks, usually in the mountains
2	Trade fair	b	Tour or excursion that leaves in the morning and returns the same evening
3	Study tour	c	Visiting the famous places in a city or town
4	Trek	d	Trip, often to a city or countryside hotel, that includes Saturday and Sunday
5	Conference	e	Religious or artistic celebration that comes at the same time every year
6	Wedding	f	Large official meeting, often lasting several days, for members of an organization or company to discuss subjects related to their work
7	Pilgrimage	g	Large exhibition and meeting for advertising and selling a product
8	Day trip	h	Visit organized by an airline or tourist resort, etc. where tour operators and journalists can get to know the facilities and services offered
9	Festival	i	Trip to a country or an area that includes visits, lectures, and classes
10	Weekend break	j	Journey or holiday given to a worker or group of workers as a reward for good work
11	Familiarization (or 'fam') trip	k	Travel to an important religious place
12	Incentive tour	l	Ceremony where two people get married

2 What is the purpose of each of the travel activities: leisure, business, or VFR?

3 Have you ever travelled for one of these activities? Tell your partner about it.

Listening

Passenger survey

1 Why do you think people would go to these places?

Argentina	Italy	Mecca
Bangkok	London	New York
Edinburgh	Madrid	Pakistan

2 🎧 Listen to the conversations at an international airport. Where are the travellers going?

3 🎧 Listen again. Complete the information in the table.

	Where from?	Destination	Purpose	Length of stay
1				
2				
3				
4				

4 🎧 Listen to the first two conversations again and complete the sentences.

1 We're collecting information _____ us monitor passenger movements.

2 We're going there _____ the Holy Shrine of the Prophet Mohammed.

3 We'll probably stay for a week or so, _____ to do some sightseeing as well afterwards.

4 I have to have my phone on _____ there's a problem at the office.

5 Are you travelling _____ trip?

The world's biggest attraction?
The Hajj is the Islamic pilgrimage
to the holy city of Mecca. There are
an estimated 1.3 billion Muslims in
the world, and during the Hajj, the
city of Mecca must cope with as
many as 4 million pilgrims.

● **Language spot**

Talking about reason

1 Match the questions in A with the answers in B.

A	B
1 Can I ask you a few questions?	a For a week or so.
2 Where are you travelling to?	b OK, thanks.
3 What is the purpose of your visit?	c Certainly.
4 Why are you visiting London?	d Yes, we want to go to Scotland.
5 How long are you planning to stay?	e For a study tour.
6 What's the reason for your trip?	f Bangkok.
7 Why don't you check?	g It's my brother's wedding.
8 Do you have any other reasons to be here?	h Business.

2 Which of the questions are asking about reason?

3 Link these sentences with *to, for, because, because of,* or *in case.* Check your answers with the listening script on p.129.

1 We're doing a passenger survey _____ help with tourism planning.

2 I've got an open return _____ they ask me to stay on.

3 We had to fly to Madrid _____ there were no direct flights available.

4 We are going to London _____ a study tour for four weeks.

5 We are here _____ we want to know about the culture, and not only _____ the famous sights.

4 Which sentence refers to a reason that *might* happen?

5 Complete these sentences spoken by other travellers at the airport.

1 We're going to Amsterdam _____ visit my sister who's just had a baby.

2 We're just waiting for our connecting flight. It's been delayed _____ technical difficulties.

3 They say the flight may be delayed, so I think I'll phone the hotel _____ we're late.

4 We're going to Rome _____ we want to see the Coliseum.

5 I'm going back to my old university _____ a special reunion. I've just bought a video camera _____ take a film of everyone.

6 Use the information in the chart in *Listening* **3** to role-play the four dialogues with a partner.

» Go to **Grammar reference** p.121

Pronunciation

1 🎧 Listen to the underlined part of each country. Are they the same?

Russia   China   Germany

2 Say the name of each country. Pay attention to the pronunciation of the part underlined.

3 🎧 Listen to the part of these words in **bold**, then write the word in the correct column.

bro**ch**ure	destina**ti**on	packa**g**e
change	Engli**sh**	passen**g**er
chart	**Eg**ypt	pilgrima**g**e
check-in	expre**ssi**on	reli**g**ious
cultural	langua**g**e	

Russia /ʃ/	**China** /tʃ/	**Germany** /dʒ/

4 Practise saying the words from each column.

Kenya offers a diverse range of interests for visitors – beaches, safaris, hiking, culture, and golf. We have it all. In a nutshell, I can say that Kenya is a wonderful place for visitors to come. Kenyan people are very friendly people.

John Muhoho
Director, CKC Tours and Travel, Nairobi

Where in the world?

1 What do you know about Kenya? What type of holiday activities does it provide?

2 What reasons would a tourist give for choosing Kenya as a holiday destination?

Listening

Interview with a Kenyan tour operator

1 🎧 Listen to the interview with John Muhoho. Complete the information and answer the questions.

1
Profile

Name	John Muhoho
Age	....
Started in tourism	....
Started CKC Tours	....

2 What does he enjoy about his job?

3 How much of his business comes from the Internet?

4 Which of these holiday activities does he mention?

beach	safari	culture
swimming	eating out	golf
shark-fishing	hiking	camel rides
sailing	mountain climbing	

2 Discuss these questions.

1 What type of tourists do you think are motivated to go to Kenya?

2 How is their motivation different from the tourists to your country?

tailor-made (adj) made for a particular person or purpose and therefore very suitable

Tourism in Africa
According to the WTO, tourist arrivals in Southern Africa will grow by 300% between 2000 and 2020. In East Africa they will grow by 170%.
South Africa is the most popular destination in the African continent with 22% of all international arrivals. Little-known African countries like Ghana and Cape Verde are predicted to be popular tourist destinations in the future.

Reading

The changing face of tourism

1 Discuss these questions with a partner.

1 How do you think tourists' reasons for travelling have changed in the last twenty or thirty years?

2 What do you think is meant by 'old' and 'new' tourism?

3 Do you think these words are related to 'old' or 'new' tourism? Use a dictionary to help you.

high-rise   package   long-haul   independent
concrete   authentic   fly-drive   ecotourism

2 Read the article to check your answers.

3 Use information from the text to complete these tables.

In Africa	Old tourism	New tourism
1 What do tourists want to do?		
2 What do tourists want to eat?		
3 Where do tourists stay?		
4 Who are the tourism employees?		

In general	Old tourism	New tourism
1 Types of holiday		
2 Length of holiday		
3 Types of activities on holiday		
4 Destinations		

Old and new tourism

In the 1980s and early 1990s, when Africans first realized that tourism could be a way out of their poverty, they built very large concrete hotels on the beaches of Kenya, South Africa, and other countries. For a time the charter flights poured in from Germany and Italy. The tourists hoped to see lions, but also wanted to lie by the pool and to eat food from their own country and enjoy the other comforts of home. The revenue from tourism rose sharply, but most of it went to international tour operators.

That was then. Fortunately, a new kind of travel is now in fashion. Today's tourists are leaving the high-rise hotels and European comforts. Instead they are looking for more authentic experiences. On the wild coast of South Africa, young tourists ride horses on unspoilt beaches and make their way through hills of subtropical vegetation. In the evening they sit round the fire and eat a traditional Xhosa meal of meat and vegetables; they listen to the local Xhosa people tell folk stories, before going to bed in simple tents and lodges. The experience is not offered by an international tour operator but by the Xhosa themselves. The Xhosa tour guides are paid two and a half times the average rate of pay.

The change from 'old tourism' to 'new tourism' did not happen suddenly. Interest in the traditional two-week sun and sea package holiday fell gradually towards the end of the last century. Individual tailor-made or independent holidays – such as fly-drive – have steadily become more popular. Nowadays people are taking shorter yet more diverse holidays. Long-haul flights are increasing and are making faraway places easier to get to. More and more tourists are looking for adventure, activity, and authenticity. Adventure travel, ecotourism, cultural tours, and sports vacations are taking people to more exotic destinations: China, the Maldives, Botswana, Vanuatu.

● Language spot

Describing trends

1 Look at these sentences from the text. Which ones describe

1 a current trend?
2 a past trend?
3 a trend from the past to the present?

a The revenue from tourism rose sharply.
b Today's tourists are leaving the high-rise hotels and European comforts.
c Interest in the traditional two-week sun and sea package holiday fell gradually towards the end of the last century.
d Individual tailor-made or independent holidays – such as fly-drive – have steadily become more popular.
e Nowadays people are taking shorter yet more diverse holidays.
f Long-haul flights are increasing and are making faraway places easier to get to.

2 Which tense is used in each sentence?

3 Can you find any other examples of current trends in the text?

4 Divide these verbs into two groups: go up [▲] and go down [▼].

rise
decrease
grow
increase
fall
drop

5 Put these adverbs in order – from small change to big change.

dramatically   steadily
gradually   sharply

6 Use the graphs to write sentences about the current trends in 1 – 6.
Start each sentence with: *The number of …*

EXAMPLE
The number of people taking package holidays is decreasing sharply.

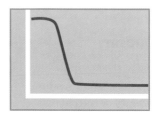

1 package holidays

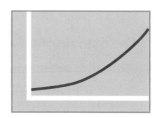

2 weekend city breaks

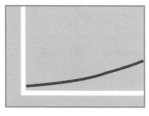

3 long-haul flights

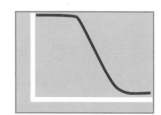

4 beach holidays

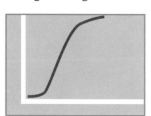

5 online holiday bookings

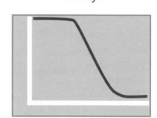

6 High Street travel agents

>> Go to **Grammar reference** p.121

Find out

1 Have there been similar changes in tourism in your country or region?

2 What was tourism in your country like (a) twenty years ago, (b) ten years ago?

3 How can you find out? Who can you ask?

4 What are the main reasons why tourists come to your country or region now?

5 Use the information you have found out to make a list of 'old' and 'new' tourism features in your country or region.

Writing

Your country or region

Use the information from *Find out* to write a short article – with graphs and charts if appropriate – about trends in 'old' and 'new' tourism in your country or region.

Speaking

Changes in tourist motivation

Work in pairs. You are going to look at two surveys on the main reasons given by tourists for their holiday. One is from 1986 and one is current. Student A, look at p.110. Student B, look at p.116.

1 Find out what, if anything, your survey says about
  1 the main reason for holiday travel
  2 attitudes to food and eating
  3 the importance of having fun
  4 the importance of weather and nature
  5 wanting new experiences
  6 meeting people and being with people.

2 Tell your partner and compare answers.

3 Look at the two surveys together. Can you identify any trends in tourist motivation?

Customer care

'We know what you want ...'

WE KNOW WHAT YOU WANT, EVEN IF YOU DON'T KNOW YOURSELF!

Staff working in tourism must be able to understand the different reasons why tourists have come on holiday. It is important to get to know your customers. Find out why they've come on holiday, what they want to do, and then help them to achieve their dreams.
Tourism Training Journal

1 Do you agree that people working in tourism should help tourists and visitors to 'achieve their dreams'? Or should they leave them alone?

2 What questions could you ask to find out why a tourist has come on holiday and what they want to do?

Checklist

Assess your progress in this unit. Tick (✓) the statements which are true.

  I can talk about purpose and reason

  I can understand a simple passenger survey

  I can describe past and current trends in tourism and tourist motivation

  I can read articles about changes in tourist motivation

Key words

Specialist industry terms
business tourism
ecotourism
fam trip (familiarization trip)
incentive tour
leisure tourism
VFR (visiting friends and relatives)

Nouns
concrete
conference
day trip
fly-drive holiday
motivation
pilgrimage
safari
study tour
trade fair
trek
trend
wedding
weekend break

Adjectives
authentic
high-rise
long-haul

Next stop

1 How did you book your last holiday?

2 Think of a travel agency you know. What kind of holidays do they specialize in?

5 Travel agencies

Take off

1 Which travel agency sells more holidays?

2 What sort of message do you think each window gives to people in the street?

3 What kind of holidays do these two travel agencies sell? Who do you think their clients are?

Listening

All in a day's work

1 Look at the typical travel agency products and services. Which of them are free, and which of them does the travel agent make money from?

1 Advice on visa and passport applications
2 Airline tickets
3 Brochures for tour operators
4 Coach tours and trips
5 Foreign currency and traveller's cheques
6 Hotel bookings
7 Package holidays
8 Train tickets
9 Transport information
10 Travel insurance

2 🎧 Listen to these customers. Which product or service do they want?

Speaker	Product / Service
1	
2	
3	
4	
5	

Reading

The sales process

Read the article.

1   In which stage does a sales consultant do most of the talking?

2   In which stage does a sales consultant have to listen most carefully?

3   Can you think of any other ways of raising customer awareness?

4   If customers are looking at brochures, why should you leave them alone?

5   Features, advantages, or benefits – which is the hardest for a sales consultant to explain to a customer?

6   The last two stages are not described in the article. What do you think happens in each stage?

Six steps to successful selling

TOP SALES TIPS

Your job as a travel agency sales consultant is to help your customers to choose their next holiday. This is a skilled job, and in order to do it well, you need to follow an established routine called the sales process.

Stage 1

To begin any sales process, it is important to raise your customer's awareness of the products your agency offers. Adverts in the agency window, for example, attract people's attention, and may bring them into the shop.

Stage 2

This is possibly the most important stage in sales. Many people are nervous about buying because they think that sales consultants only want to get their money. From the very first moment with a new client, you need to convince them that you are really interested in helping them find the right holiday.

Of course, sometimes people go into a travel agency just to browse through the brochures. In this case, do not stand next to them and ask questions. Let them know you are there, but leave them alone. Give them time.

5 closing the sale

6 after-sales service

1 raising awareness

4 presenting products

2 establishing rapport

3 investigating needs

Stage 3

When a customer asks for help or information, we move on to the next stage – investigating the customer's needs. This is also an important part of the sales process; it is only when you have a clear idea about where a client wants to go, when they want to travel, who with, and so on, that you can select the best products for them.

Stage 4

When you have selected the most suitable products, you need to present them in terms of:

Features – these are what a holiday <u>has</u>, such as the hotel facilities, transfers from the airport, excursions, etc.

Advantages – these are what make the holiday <u>better</u> than other similar holidays. The fact that the price of a holiday includes all the excursions, or all your bar costs, for example, would be an advantage.

Benefits – why a particular feature is good for the customer you are talking to at that moment.

At this point in the process many customers will want time to think. The best thing to do is to get their contact details and invite them to take the brochures home and browse through them. If you have done a good job of presenting the product, they will probably be back a few days later.

Stage 5

When the customer returns to your agency …

Vocabulary

Sales terms

1 Match the words in the list with their definitions.

advantage   benefit   consultant
awareness   browse   convince

1 a person who gives information or advice in business
2 a useful, positive effect that something has
3 knowing about something and probably being interested in it
4 something that helps or that gives a better chance of success
5 to spend time looking at something without a clear idea of what you want
6 to succeed in making somebody believe something

2 Which words are nouns and which are verbs?

3 Complete the sentences using the words in the list.

1 A good _____ does not necessarily know the answers to every question, but does know where to find the answer.

2 Adverts on TV and in magazines are used to create _____ of new products.

3 The _____ of using a travel agent is that they can help you to find the best holiday.

4 The main _____ of learning English is that most people in tourism speak it.

5 There is so much information to _____ through on the Internet that it is easy not to find what you want.

4 Use your dictionary. Find three more terms in the article. For each one, write out the definition from your dictionary. Ask your partner to find the word in the article.

Listening

A new customer

1 🎧 Karl and Anita want to go to Australia. They go to a travel agent's for advice. Listen to their conversation and answer the questions.

1 Which two stages of the sales process do you hear?
2 Does the sales consultant finish the second stage?

2 🎧 Listen again and write T (true) or F (false).
Karl and Anita want

1 to travel around Australia with their daughter
2 a package holiday for the three of them
3 to fly to Adelaide
4 to travel out to Australia in July
5 to stay for longer than three weeks
6 to stay in Melbourne for twelve hours.

3 Do you think the sales consultant did her job well in these stages? Why / Why not?

● Language spot

'Open' and 'closed' questions

1 🎧 Listen again and complete the following questions.
1 Can I _____ you?
2 Were you _____ about a _____?
3 Where is _____ daughter, by the _____?
4 When _____ did you want to _____?

Travel sales commissions
Travel agencies receive commission for the sale of different products. For package holidays this is usually 10%, for traveller's cheques 1% and for travel insurance 35–40%.

Commission on air ticket sales used to be around 8% but is now usually 0%, so the travel agency charges the customer for this sale instead.

Customer care

Identifying needs

Customer: An individual with a unique set of characteristics who buys or uses tourism products and services. Customers have very different needs and it is a travel agent's job to find out what these are.

1 What sort of characteristics can you identify as soon as a customer walks into your agency?

2 What other characteristics do you need to determine? How will you find these out?

2 Which of the questions in **1** can you answer with *Yes* or *No*?

3 How would you answer the other two questions?

4 Questions can be 'open' or 'closed'. What do you think this means?

5 Convert the following closed questions into open ones.

1 Do you want to be in Australia for a month?
2 Are you interested in visiting Sydney?
3 Do you want to stay in hotels?
4 Are you travelling in a group?
5 Can you go in the autumn?
6 Are you willing to pay a lot of money?
7 Do you go there every day?

» Go to **Grammar reference** p.122

Speaking

Investigating a client's needs

1 Work in threes. Take turns to be the sales consultant and the customers. Sales consultant, look at p.110. Customers, look at p.115.

2 The sales consultant should complete the initial enquiry form where possible.

3 When each conversation is finished, check that the information is correct.

TRAVELWELL TOURS

Initial Enquiry Form

Customer name

Booked before with TT?   Yes / No

Contact telephone / fax / email:

Holiday type: Adventure / Beach / Cruise / Family /
Historic / Nightlife / Tour

Dates: Departure   Return

Size of party:

Type of party: Married couple / Family / Friends / Other

Accommodation preferences:

Meal preferences:

Needs / Interests:

Other requirements / useful details:

It's my job

Michaela Cambelová

Michaela Cambelová works in a busy travel agency in Prague. Think about the stages in the sales process. Find out which stage Michaela is best at.

Q Michaela, what do you like about being a sales consultant?

A I like the contact with the clients. People are very different, and for me, finding out what each customer is like and what they want is fascinating.

Q What skills does a good sales consultant need?

A Patience, psychology, and a comprehensive knowledge of the products available.

Q Why do you need psychology?

A You've got to know when a customer is ready for your help, when they need more time, or when they're ready to buy.

Q And knowledge of the product?

A Well, above all, you've got to know what's inside the brochures, and not just what's on the page.

Q What do you mean?

A Well, it's not the same talking about a place in a brochure as talking about a place you've been to, or that a client has told you about. You're only as good as the information you've got, so you need to read, to

travel, and to keep in touch with your clients.

Q What about the Internet for information?

A It's really important. But you've got to find information quickly and efficiently. There's so much on the Internet that if your reading skills are poor you'll need all day to examine each site. And you haven't got all day.

Find out

How good is the service in your local travel agencies? Think of a holiday or a journey you would like to go on. Visit a local travel agency and ask for information. During your visit carefully observe

1 the shop window (Attractive? Original? etc.)
2 the interior (Organized? Spacious? etc.)
3 the greeting (Immediate? Warm? etc.)
4 the sales consultant's manner (Friendly? Attentive? etc.)
5 the result of the visit (As expected? Better than expected?)

Writing

A report on a travel agency

Write up your experience at the local travel agency as a report. Use the following structure.

Title:	*Travel agency quality assessment*
Assessor:	Put your name and contact details
Agency:	Put the name of the agency you visited
Date of visit:	Put the full date of your visit
Address:	Put the contact details of your agency
Features:	Write one or two sentences describing and evaluating the window. Do the same for the interior, the travel agent's greeting, and their manner.
Result:	Write one or two sentences describing and evaluating the result.
Grade:	Give each feature a mark from 0 (minimum) to 5 (maximum)

Window ☐   Interior ☐   Greeting ☐
Manner ☐   Result ☐

Where do visitors to Australia come from?

1	New Zealand	6	Korea
2	Japan	7	China
3	UK	8	Malaysia
4	USA	9	Germany
5	Singapore	10	Hong Kong

Listening

Presenting a product

TOUR NAME	# OF DAYS	DESTINATION
All Australia	19	Melbourne – Great Ocean Road – Kangaroo Island – Adelaide – Uluru (Ayers Rock) – Alice Springs – Palm Valley – Darwin – Kakadu National Park – Cairns – Great Barrier Reef – Brisbane – Sydney
Australia's Best	13	Melbourne – Alice Springs – Uluru (Ayers Rock) – the Olgas – Cairns – Great Barrier Reef – Kuranda Scenic Railway – Brisbane – Sydney
East Coast Highlights	9	Melbourne – Cairns – Kuranda Scenic Railway – Great Barrier Reef – Sydney
Reef and Rainforest	7	Cairns – Great Barrier Reef – Daintree National Park – Dunk Island – Kuranda
Red Centre and the West	8	Alice Springs – Macdonnell Ranges – the Olgas – Uluru (Ayers Rock) – Kalgoorlie – Perth – the Pinnacles

Title: A STRA IA • tours

1 🎧 Listen to the travel agent presenting two products to Karl and Anita.

1 Which place does Karl want to visit?
2 Which place does Anita want to visit?
3 Which two tours does the travel agent recommend?

2 🎧 Listen again. For each of the two tours recommended, note down

1 the length of the tour
2 the types of transport each tour uses
3 the accommodation and meals included.

3 🎧 Listen again and complete the sentences.

1 … they have two in Australia that you _____ think about, in _____ _____.

2 … full-board option with all the meals. But if I were _____ , _____ _____ half-board.

3 Well then, why don't you _____ _____ the Australia's Best tour?

● Language spot

Suggestions and advice

1 Match the expressions for advice on the left with possible continuations on the right.

1	In my opinion, you should …	a	I'd look on the Internet.
2	Have you thought about …	b	is to look on the Internet.
3	How about …	c	look on the Internet?
4	If I were you …	d	look on the Internet.
5	Why don't you …	e	looking on the Internet?
6	Your best option …	f	the Internet?

2 Now do the same with these expressions.

1	Have you thought about …	a	going in the autumn?
2	How about …	b	is to hire a car.
3	If I were you …	c	taking the coach to the airport?
4	Why don't you …	d	take a look at these brochures?
5	In my opinion, you should …	e	I'd ask a travel agent.
6	Your best option …	f	travel overnight on the train.

3 Work in groups of four.

Each person should think of two travel decisions a visitor to your country or region might want advice on.

Take turns to ask your partners for advice.

Give marks (a) for each different advice expression used correctly, and (b) for each original piece of advice given.

>> Go to **Grammar reference** p.122

benefit (v) to produce a good or useful effect

career (n) the series of jobs that sb has in a particular area of work

expertise (n) a high level of special knowledge or skill

myth (n) an idea or story which many people believe but that does not exist or is false

value (n) sth that is well worth the money it costs

Pronunciation

1 🎧 Listen to the letters of the alphabet and their pronunciation. Write them in the right column.

Pronunciation						
/eɪ/	/iː/	/e/	/aɪ/	/əʊ/	/uː/	/aː/
a	b	f	i	o	q	r

2 Practise saying the letters column by column.

3 Say the alphabet.

Speaking

Suggesting alternatives and making a recommendation

1 Work in pairs. Take turns to be the sales consultant and the customers. Student A, look at p.110. Student B, look at p.115. Act out a conversation in a travel agent's, going through the three stages of the sales process you have seen in this unit: establishing rapport, investigating needs, and presenting possible products. Finish your conversation by getting your partner to spell out their name.

2 Now think about your own area of the world. Your partner will be a customer who does not know the area at all. Establish rapport, investigate needs, make suitable recommendations, and then present possible products. And don't forget to get your client's name!

3 Record your conversation and give it to your teacher to mark for language and pronunciation.

Reading

The impact of the Internet

Many holidays are now sold on the Internet. Travel agencies around the world are worried about this and are trying to explain why they are still important. The *American Society of Travel Agents* (ASTA) is using the Internet to do this!

1 Here are five popular myths about travel agencies.

1 all travel agencies are the same so it does not matter which one a client uses

2 because of the Internet, people will not use travel agencies in the future

TRAVEL AGENCY myths AND REALities

Myth: Travel agents are just glorified sellers of airline tickets.

Reality: Travel agents are professionals who provide **value** by helping save time and money. They act as travel consultants, offering personal service for their clients. Clients who turn to an ASTA travel agent want the advice and **expertise** of a professional who

- analyses current promotions
- explains the small print, such as cancellation charges and restrictions
- makes recommendations on travel options
- gets problems solved.

Myth: The Internet will replace the need for travel agents.

Reality: When it comes to booking travel, travel agents are experienced professionals. Travel agents sell

- 87% of all cruises
- 81% of all tours and packages

3   travel agencies are against travel products being on the Internet

4   travel agencies are just *shops* that sell tickets for planes

5   young people do not use travel agents

Four of these myths are discussed in the ASTA article. Which four?

2   What is the reality for each myth according to ASTA?

3   How would you answer the fifth myth from ASTA's point of view?

51% of all airline tickets

47% of all hotels

45% of all car rentals.

The Internet is a valuable resource, but it cannot replace the expertise, guidance, and personal service of a travel agent.

Myth: Travel agents do not support use of the Internet.

Reality: Both consumers and travel professionals **benefit** from the Internet. The Internet gives travellers the ability to shop for attractive offers or packages. It has also helped many travel agencies, hotels, resorts, and other travel-related suppliers to grow by bringing in business through websites.

Myth: Young people do not understand or value the services of a travel agent.

Reality: Yes, they do. Of the people who use travel agents

43% are age 35–54

33% are Generation X and Y travellers, age 18–34.

One of the winners of ASTA's and Hyatt Hotel's 'Best Practices Program' has made a point to educate students about the adventure of travel and of being a travel agent as a **career**. This process has made young people aware of the expertise required to be a professional travel agent.

Checklist

Assess your progress in this unit. Tick (✓) the statements which are true.

I can investigate a client's holiday needs

I can make suggestions and give advice to a new customer

I can make a report on travel agency quality and features

I can pronounce the letters of the alphabet and spell aloud

I can understand texts about travel agency work today

Key words

Nouns

advantage	product
advice	rapport
awareness	requirement
benefit	sales consultant
contact details	sales process
feature	travel insurance
foreign currency	visa
initial enquiry form	

Adjectives

skilled

Verbs

browse

convince

establish (rapport)

investigate (needs, requirements)

present (a product)

raise (customer awareness)

Next stop

1   How do you prefer to travel – by car, by coach, by train, by boat, … ? Why?

2   What was the most uncomfortable journey you have ever made? Tell your partner.

3   If you could travel around the world, but you couldn't fly, how would you go?

6 Transport in tourism

Take off

1 Look at the map below. Which countries does each route pass through?

2 Choose one of the journeys. What type of transport could be used on each stage?

3 Which route would you prefer to take? Why? What would you hope to do and see? Exchange ideas with a partner.

Vocabulary

Transport words

1 Use words from the table to complete the text on 'transport for tourism'.

	Method of travel	Journey types	Transport types	Places and features	Tourism professionals
	Air	flight (long-haul) (short-haul)	airplane / jet light aircraft helicopter	airport terminal runway	pilot flight attendant
	Water	cruise crossing	cruise ship liner ferry hovercraft hydrofoil	port harbour cabin pier	steward purser
	Land	ride journey drive tour	train coach bus car motorbike bicycle	station carriage terminus motorway track	guard driver conductor tour guide

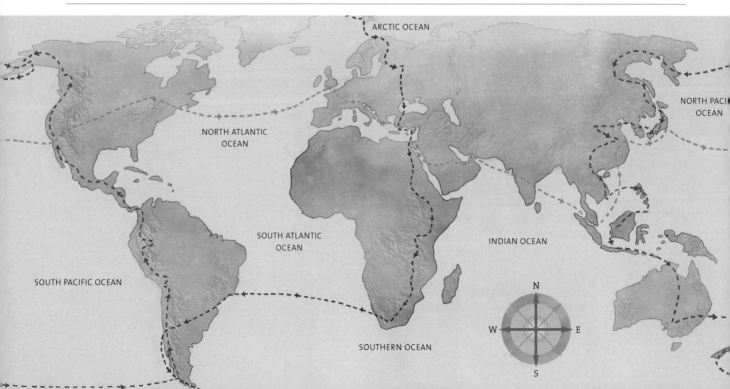

In this unit
- types of transport and journeys
- describing transport
- comparing types of transport
- describing timetables

Inside tourism: transport for tourism

Transport for tourists can be divided into three main categories: journeys by air, journeys on water, and journeys on _____¹. Within each category there are several types of transport.

Air travel usually means a short-haul or _____² international _____³, operating from large _____⁴, which in big cities often have more than one _____⁵ building. But in some more remote places there may be little more than a small airstrip with only one simple _____⁶ for planes to land and take off. At some tourist destinations air transport may include short transfers or sightseeing trips by _____⁷.

Journeys on water can include luxury _____⁸, which take tourists on all-inclusive holidays of three days or more, visiting a number of different locations. Passengers sleep in _____⁹, and have a full range of services on board. They are looked after by a team of _____¹⁰, with a _____¹¹ in overall charge of tourist services. Ferry _____¹² are usually much shorter journeys connecting two points of land or going between islands. The ferries will stop at a large _____¹³ or a small _____¹⁴.

Land travel is probably the most diverse category. It includes rail journeys by _____¹⁵, departing from a large _____¹⁶ and stopping at _____¹⁷ en route. Passengers sit in separate _____¹⁸ or coaches. The most common form of transport by road for tourists, if they don't have their own car, are also called _____¹⁹. These vehicles can either travel from city to city along fast _____²⁰ (or sometimes quieter roads), or they can be used for transfers from airports and other smaller journeys. Very often they are used for sightseeing trips when as well as a driver there will be a _____²¹ to tell the passengers about the sights.

2 Can you add any more words to the table? Look back at the previous units.

3 Which sections would you put these words in?

taxi	marina
ticket collector	jeep
hire car	service station
captain	scenic route
freeway	shuttle
yacht	tunnel

4 How do tourists use the different types of transport? Put the journey and transport types (from columns 1 and 2 of the table) into the categories below.

1. to and from destination only (e.g. *international flight*)
2. at destination only (e.g. *taxi ride from airport*)
3. as a main feature of the holiday (e.g. *sightseeing helicopter ride*)

5 Which types of transport have you used? Think about the best and worst journeys you have ever made. Exchange ideas with a partner.

Find out

What do you really know about transport in your country? With a partner, try to guess the facts in the table.

When you have made your predictions, research websites of national transport carriers and find the actual figures. Report back in class. How close were your predictions?

Your country:	Prediction	Actual
No. of city / town bus stations		
No. of city / town train stations		
No. of passenger airports		
No. of kilometres of road		
No. of kilometres of rail tracks		
No. of flights per day		

Transport in the USA

Number of cities or towns served by different transport types		Percentage of person-trips (intercity)	
Bus stations	4,200	Car	80%
Train stations	600	Air	17%
Airports	750	Train	1%
		Bus (BrE = coach)	1%

Pronunciation

1 🎧 Look at the words about transport. Listen to their pronunciation. Write three words in each column.

clean	ferry	leisure	safe	train
easy	jet	plane	scenic	

ten /e/	**see** /iː/	**day** /eɪ/

2 Which column has the shortest vowel sounds?

3 Practise the words. Remember to make them short / long as appropriate.

4 🎧 Now do the same with these words. Listen and write them in the right column.

car	drive	guard	harbour	track
craft	fast	guide	ride	

hat /æ/	**arm** /ɑː/	**five** /aɪ/

Vocabulary

Adjectives describing transport

1 Find pairs of opposites from the adjectives in the list.

boring	expensive
cheap	exciting
clean	fast
comfortable	punctual
crowded	safe
dangerous	quiet
difficult	slow
dirty	uncomfortable
easy	unpunctual

2 Choose three adjectives that describe what is most important for tourists when travelling. Are they different for different types of transport?
Tourists want planes to be _____ and _____, but they don't want them to be _____ .

● Language spot
Comparing things

1 Complete these sentences with the correct form of the adjectives: *fast*, *easy*, or *comfortable*.

1 Trains are _____ than buses, but planes are the _____ .

2 The _____ way to buy a ticket is to go online.

3 It's _____ to travel first class than economy.

4 Helicopters aren't as _____ as jet planes.

5 Travelling by bus is usually less _____ than travelling by train.

2 What are the rules for comparing adjectives? Complete the table.

Adjectives	Example	Comparing two things	Comparing more than two things
One syllable	cheap	X is cheaper than Y *or* Y isn't as cheap as X	Z is the cheapest
Two syllables ending in *y*	easy		
Two or more syllables	comfortable		
Irregular adjectives	good bad		

3 In pairs, compare the following.

1 ferries / cruise ships
2 trains / coaches / cars
3 working as a pilot / working as a ticket collector
4 the most convenient ways to get around a city

» Go to **Grammar reference** p.122

There are 4 million miles
(6.4 million kilometres) of road, 51,000 of
which are 'scenic' roads.

There are 22,000 miles
(35,400 kilometres) of train track.

There are approximately 25,000 flights a day.

Speaking

What is most important for tourists when travelling?

1 Work in groups. Look at the factors that affect a tourist's enjoyment of a journey. Can you add any more?

At the airport	On a train	On a long coach journey	On a four-hour ferry crossing
Quick check-in	Punctuality	A window seat	A private cabin
Good restaurants	Interesting passengers to talk to	On-board toilets	Opportunity to buy tax-free goods
Thorough security check	Comfortable seats	Safe driver	Calm sea

2 Discuss which you think are the most important features for a tourist on each journey. Put them in order.

3 Compare your ideas with other groups. Give arguments why you think your order is correct.
The most important thing on a coach journey is …
Comfort is more important than _____ because …

Customer care

Exceeding expectations

In tourism the most important thing is not just to meet expectations, but to exceed them.

Do you agree?

Hotels try to exceed expectations in many ways. How can we exceed expectations in the transport sector? Think about the different transport types – air, sea / river, rail, and road.

Listening

Transport systems and cable cars in San Francisco

🎧 Listen to the recorded information line on transport (AmE = transportation) in San Francisco.

1 Which of the following transport types does the information line describe?

ferries	trains	bike rental
cruises	airplanes	coach tours
buses	helicopter rides	walking tours
metro	cable cars	car hire

2 Complete the information sheet on cable cars.

FACT SHEET

First introduced: ....

Number of lines: ....

Hours of operation: ....

Days of operation: ....

Cost of single journey: ....

Board at: ....

Amtrak has 68,000 passengers per day, which means 25 million passengers per year.

Amtrak was established in 1971 with 25 employees; it now has 22,000 across the USA.

Reading

San Francisco transport timetables and schedules

Look at the three timetables for (a) trips to Alcatraz and Muir Woods, (b) BART trains to and from San Francisco airport, and (c) Amtrak train services between Los Angeles and San Francisco.

a

BLUE AND GOLD TOURS

Alcatraz
Visit the famous island prison of Alcatraz, only accessible by ferry

FISHERMAN'S WHARF, PIER 41 (DAILY)

Depart Pier 41		Depart Alcatraz	
9:30 am	12:15 pm	9:50 am	1:15 pm
10:15 am	12:45 pm	10:35 am	1:45 pm
10:45 am	1:15 pm	11:10 am	2:15 pm
11:15 am	1:45 pm	11:45 am	2:45 pm
11:45 am	2:15 pm	12:15 am	3:20 pm
		12:45 pm	3:50 pm
			4:30 pm

Access: SEAT (Sustainable Easy Access Transport) is available for wheelchair users and visitors with a mobility need who are unable to walk up the quarter-mile, 12% grade hill.

Children under 14 must be escorted by an adult.

Only service dogs allowed.

No bicycles or scooters allowed on island.

For Daytime Alcatraz Tours: No service Christmas Day (Dec 25) or New Year's Day (Jan 1)

For Evening Alcatraz Tours: No service Thanksgiving Day (Nov 25), Christmas Day (Dec 25) or New Year's Day (Jan 1)

Muir Woods
See the fabulous redwood trees and walk the coastal trails

FISHERMAN'S WHARF, PIER 41 (DAILY)*

9:15 am   2:15 pm

Muir Woods Package includes round-trip bus shuttle or the option to return to Pier 41 via the Sausalito Ferry and 45–60 minutes in the woods

Total tour length approximately 3.5 hours

Muir Woods Tour does not operate during inclement weather: check with ticket booth on day-of for schedule. Service dogs allowed. No bicycles or scooters allowed.

*No service Christmas Day (Dec 25)

b

BART (Bay Area Rapid Transit):
Services between downtown San Francisco and SFO (San Francisco International Airport)

Trains depart every 15 to 20 minutes and take approximately 30 minutes.

		Inbound		Outbound	
		SFO	Powell St	Powell St	SFO
Weekdays	First train	4:10 am	4:39 am	4:57 am	5:27 am
	Last train	11:51 pm	12:20 am	1:04 am	1:34 am
Saturday	First train	6:05 am	6:34 am	6:34 am	7:04 am
	Last train	11:51 pm	12:20 am	1:04 am	1:34 am
Sunday	First train	8:05 am	8:34 am	8:29 am	9:04 am
	Last train	11:51 pm	12:20 am	1:04 am	1:34 am

Notes:
Bicycles are not allowed during rush hours
Free parking is available at most BART stations
Discount fares available to seniors and people with disabilities

c

Amtrak train services
between Los Angeles and San Francisco

Los Angeles	Dep	1:25a	7:45a	10:45a	1:15p
Bakersfield	Arr	4:40a	10:00a	1:00p	3:30p

		#711	#713	#715	#717
Bakersfield	Dep	4:55a	10:15a	1:15p	3:45p
Fresno	Arr	6:46a	12:16p	3:16p	5:46p
Fresno	Dep	6:50a	12:20p	3:20p	5:50p
Stockton	Arr	8:54a	2:26p	5:26p	8:01p
Stockton	Dep	8:58a	2:30p	5:30p	8:05p
Emeryville	Arr	10:43a	4:13p	7:13p	9:48p

Emeryville	Dep	10:47a	4:17p	7:17p	9:52p
San Francisco	Arr	11:20a	4:50p	7:40p	10:15p

Notes: Services operate daily. Bicycles can be carried on all trains. Buses have some bicycle space but this is limited. Special discounts for frequent riders

1 Which trip (or trips)

1 is by ferry?
2 runs every day?
3 involves more than one form of transport?
4 provides special transport for people in wheelchairs?
5 offers cheaper fares for the elderly or disabled?
6 offers cheaper tickets for people who travel a lot?
7 allows bicycles?
8 does not allow bicycles?
9 does not operate in bad weather?
10 allows dogs?

2 Match the two halves of these exchanges.

1	Where does the ferry for Alcatraz leave from?	a It leaves at 2.15.
2	Can I take my bicycle on the ferry?	b It takes about 20 minutes.
3	How frequent are the ferries?	c No, they're not allowed.
4	When is the last ferry back?	d It departs from Pier 41.
5	How long does the ferry take?	e They leave approximately every 30 minutes.

● Language spot

Describing a timetable

A number of different language areas are important when we describe a timetable

Present Simple
The train *leaves* at 9.15 a.m.

Prepositions
The train leaves *at* 9.15 a.m.

Time phrase
Trains depart *every 30 minutes*.

Modals of possibility, obligation, and prohibition
Bicycles *can* be carried on all trains.
Children under 14 *must* be escorted by an adult.

1 Can you find other examples of these language areas in the listening on cable cars? Look at the listening script on p.131.

2 Complete this paragraph giving recorded information on the Alcatraz ferry service.

Ferries for Alcatraz _____¹ approximately _____² 30 minutes. The first ferry _____³ _____⁴ Pier 41 _____⁵ 9:30 a.m., and the last ferry is _____⁶ _____⁷. Return ferries run throughout the day. The last ferry _____⁸ Alcatraz _____⁹ _____¹⁰ p.m. Services are _____¹¹ except for Christmas Day and New Year's Day. You _____¹² take bicycles or scooters on to the island.

>> Go to **Grammar reference** p.123

Speaking

Timetable information

Work in groups. Half of you are tourists asking about cable cars in San Francisco. The other half will ask about Amtrak services from Los Angeles to San Francisco.

1 Think of questions you can ask a travel information officer about

- times and frequency
- first and last services
- routes
- facilities (e.g. for disabled people)
- bicycles, etc.

2 Work with someone from the other group and take turns to ask and answer each other's questions. To answer the questions you should refer to the texts, but some of the information will not be there, so you will have to think of a likely answer.

3 Return to your groups and compare answers.

Writing

Transport and timetable information

Prepare a website about transport in your city or region. It should include the following sections.

- A general introduction to transport services
- Getting to and from the nearest airport
- A brief description of each of the different types of transport, including advantages, frequency, hours of operation, and any restrictions and regulations

Where in the world?

1 Look at the picture of a modern cruise ship. Find

1 five places where passengers can eat or drink
2 four sporting activities passengers can do
3 three places that are suitable for children
4 two places where passengers can dance
5 one place where you would most like to be.

2 Which of the facilities do you think you would use most as a passenger?

3 In which of the facilities would you most like to work?

4 In which of the facilities would you least like to work?

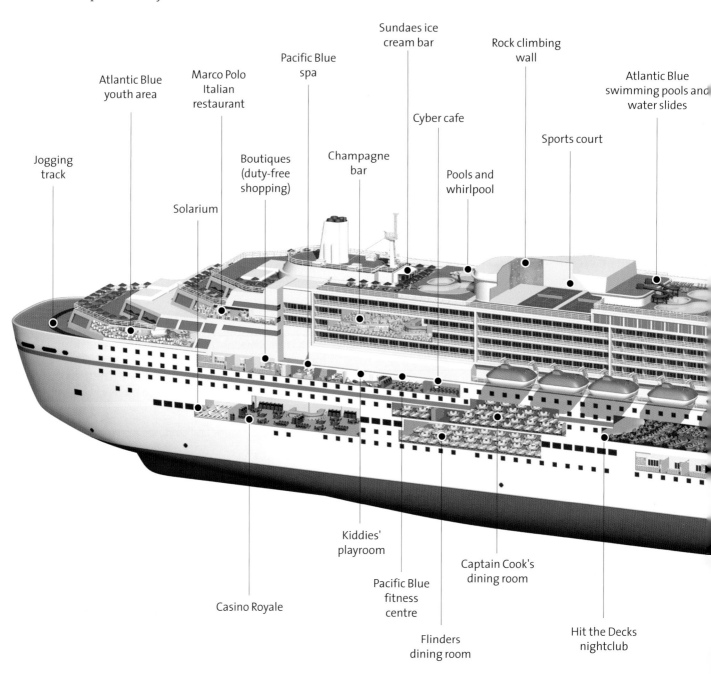

Jogging track

Atlantic Blue youth area

Marco Polo Italian restaurant

Pacific Blue spa

Sundaes ice cream bar

Rock climbing wall

Atlantic Blue swimming pools and water slides

Cyber cafe

Sports court

Solarium

Boutiques (duty-free shopping)

Champagne bar

Pools and whirlpool

Kiddies' playroom

Pacific Blue fitness centre

Captain Cook's dining room

Hit the Decks nightclub

Casino Royale

Flinders dining room

Listening

A cruise ship worker

1 Work in pairs. Discuss the questions.

1   What do you think it is like to work on a cruise ship?

2   What would the living conditions and hours be like?

3   What do you think are the advantages and disadvantages of working on a cruise ship?

2 🎧 Listen to Steve Fairclough from Manchester and answer the questions.

1   What jobs and training did he have before working on a cruise ship?

2   Apart from a letter, what two things did he send when he applied for a job?

3   Where did he join his first cruise ship?

4   What does he say are the disadvantages of the job?

5   What are the advantages?

Checklist

Assess your progress in this unit. Tick (✓) the statements which are true.

I can discuss and compare different types of transport

I can discuss customer preferences when travelling

I can understand and describe timetables

Key words

Type of transport	Jobs in transport
cable car	conductor
cruise ship	guard
ferry	purser
hovercraft	steward
jeep	ticket collector
shuttle	
yacht	

Other nouns

cabin	runway
carriage	service station
marina	terminal
motorway (AmE = freeway)	terminus
pier	track

Next stop

1   Have you ever stayed in a hotel or other form of tourist / traveller accommodation? Where and when? What was it like?

2   What do you think are the best and worst jobs in a hotel?

The Greens golf course

19th Hole golf bar

Sparkles dancing lounge

Theatre

Trade Winds piano bar

Amerigo's fast food

Writing bank

1 Personal statement

Personal statements are a way of stating your interests, skills, experience, and development needs in your education and training. They are useful for seeing what your strengths are and for seeing what you need to improve. You can also send them to potential employers, together with a CV.

1 Read the personal statement for Gabriela Cometa.

1 Which of these jobs do you think she would be interested in?

hotel receptionist
children's entertainer
flight attendant
tour guide
nanny

2 Which of her skills and qualities will be most useful for this job?

2 Write a personal statement for yourself.

Name: Gabriela Cometa

I am interested in tourism because it is an exciting industry and it will give me the opportunity to travel to other countries.

> Describing general interests

The sector of tourism I want to work in is accommodation and catering, particularly child care and entertainment.

> Describing specific interests

My skills and qualities include the following: I am very friendly, hardworking, and creative. I am good at looking after children and I enjoy working with people. I am willing to work long hours. I am quite good at languages. My English is intermediate level, and I also speak a little French.

> Describing skills and qualifications

I have had some training and experience in tourism already. This includes an initial tourism training certificate, and experience with child care.

> Describing experience and training

I need to improve my English language skills in a number of ways. I need to get more practice at speaking English. My grammar is good, but I need to use it more fluently. I also need to learn vocabulary for tourism.

> Describing language ability

Name:

I am interested in tourism because …

The sector of tourism I want to work in is …

My skills and qualities include the following:

I have had some training and experience in tourism already. This includes …

I need to improve my English language skills in a number of ways:

2 Letter of application

1 Read the letter of application.

  1 What job is she hoping to find?

  2 What points does she include from her Personal Statement? Are there any extra ones?

2 Look at the extracts from a summer jobs book below. Prepare a letter of application for one of them. Use the same layout and some of the same expressions as Gabriela.

EAC Activity Camps

59 George Street, Edinburgh EH2 2LQ

Multi-activity day and residential camps for children aged 5 to 16 throughout the UK. Positions available: Camp Directors, Assistant Camp Directors, Qualified Instructors (archery, swimming, football, and tennis). Accommodation and food provided. Must have all-round sporting ability and be enthusiastic. Approx. 40 hours per week. The work is hard but good fun and very rewarding. Overseas applicants welcome.

Butlins Skyline Bognor Regis

Bognor Regis, West Sussex PO21 1JJ

Summer staff required for variety of positions in following departments: Guest Catering, Accommodation, Sports and Leisure, Security, Retail, Nursery, Entertainments, Funfair, Administration, Lifeguards. Competitive rates of pay and benefits. Training available. Accommodation available.

The Manager
Sunnyside Holiday Camps
Ipswich Road
Kessingland
Suffolk NR3 7JN
UK

Gabriela Cometa
via Statuto 246
Milan 1008

15 April 2006

Dear Sir or Madam

I am writing to enquire if you have any opportunities for children's entertainers and nannies at your resort this summer.

I am eighteen years old and I am currently studying for a Diploma in Tourism at the College of Travel and Tourism in Milan. I have also worked as a part-time assistant at a local nursery. I am fully experienced in looking after babies and young children up to the age of twelve. I am able to help with babysitting, preparing children's meals, and organizing activities. I enjoy looking after children and I like working as part of a team.

My mother tongue is Italian and I have a good spoken level of English. I also speak a little French.

I would be grateful if you could send me details of any available positions, including an application form.

I look forward to hearing from you.

Yours faithfully

Gabriela Cometa

Address of company you are writing to

Your name and address

Date

Dear Sir or Madam

I am writing to …

De Vere Hotels and Leisure

2100 Daresbury Park, Warrington WA4 4BP

A highly focused company concentrating on two growth markets – hotels and health and fitness. Vacancies for Waiting Staff, Room Attendants, Porters, Bar Staff, Commis Chefs, and Casual Banqueting Staff. Must be over eighteen and available to work for a minimum of four weeks between May and October. Overseas applicants who speak English and are eligible to work in the UK may apply.

3 Email to a client

1 Look at the email.

  1 Who is it from, who is it for, and what is it about?

  2 Where is the client travelling to, and when will the client get back home?

  3 What three things does the client have to do now in response to the email?

2 Mr Kaboodvand has replied saying that he cannot leave Lima until Wednesday morning. There's a flight at 14.30h on the Wednesday. Email him to ask him to confirm that this flight is OK for him. Remind him that he still has not told you if he wants a paper ticket or an electronic one.

> Send a copy of emails to people who should know about the content.

> Make sure the subject line describes the content of the email clearly.

> Do not address a client with informal greetings like 'Hi' or 'Hello'. Use 'Dear'.

> Always refer to previous communication with the client.

> Organize your text so that it is easy to read. Leave blank lines between different parts of your message.

> If the client has to respond to your email, tell him / her what you want them to do clearly. If there is a time limit for their response, make this clear to the client, or put the word URGENT in the subject line.

> Use 'Yours sincerely' when you know the client's name. If you know the client quite well, you can use 'Kind regards' as an alternative.

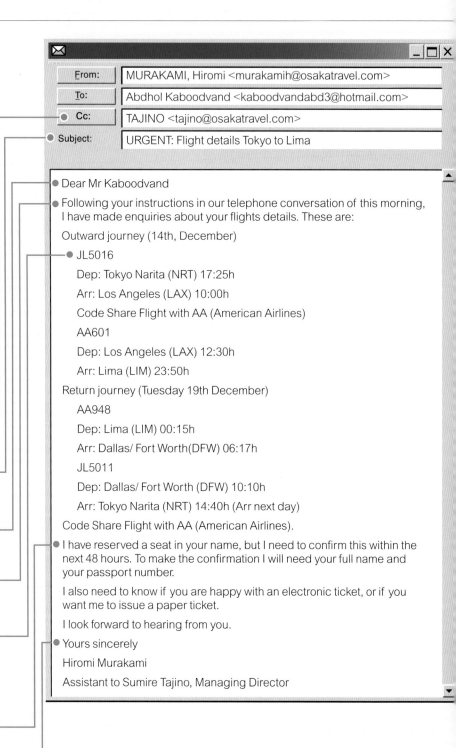

From: MURAKAMI, Hiromi <murakamih@osakatravel.com>

To: Abdhol Kaboodvand <kaboodvandabd3@hotmail.com>

Cc: TAJINO <tajino@osakatravel.com>

Subject: URGENT: Flight details Tokyo to Lima

Dear Mr Kaboodvand

Following your instructions in our telephone conversation of this morning, I have made enquiries about your flights details. These are:

Outward journey (14th, December)

JL5016

Dep: Tokyo Narita (NRT) 17:25h

Arr: Los Angeles (LAX) 10:00h

Code Share Flight with AA (American Airlines)

AA601

Dep: Los Angeles (LAX) 12:30h

Arr: Lima (LIM) 23:50h

Return journey (Tuesday 19th December)

AA948

Dep: Lima (LIM) 00:15h

Arr: Dallas/ Fort Worth(DFW) 06:17h

JL5011

Dep: Dallas/ Fort Worth (DFW) 10:10h

Arr: Tokyo Narita (NRT) 14:40h (Arr next day)

Code Share Flight with AA (American Airlines).

I have reserved a seat in your name, but I need to confirm this within the next 48 hours. To make the confirmation I will need your full name and your passport number.

I also need to know if you are happy with an electronic ticket, or if you want me to issue a paper ticket.

I look forward to hearing from you.

Yours sincerely

Hiromi Murakami

Assistant to Sumire Tajino, Managing Director

4 Email to one of your bosses

Cathie works for the travel agency *Travelweb* where she is a junior sales consultant. Her boss, Elaine Watts, asked her to find accommodation in Hanoi (Vietnam) for Professor Kate Jacoby, one of *Travelweb's* important clients. Unfortunately, Cathie discovers that the hotel the company normally uses is fully booked, and decides to get help from a friend who knows Hanoi very well. First, she writes to her boss to tell her this.

1 Read Cathie's email to Elaine. What things in the email show that Elaine is Cathie's superior?

2 Imagine you work in *Travelweb*. You have just been talking on the phone to a regular client, Dr Leshem. The doctor has made a mistake with the dates he gave you for a flight you booked for him. Unfortunately, the ticket has already been issued, and the ticket conditions do not officially accept changes. In this situation technically there is nothing you can do to help Dr Leshem, and he will have to buy a new ticket. However, you have friend at KLM, the company that issued the ticket, and you want to ring her and try to get her to help you. Email your boss, Elaine, and ask her permission.

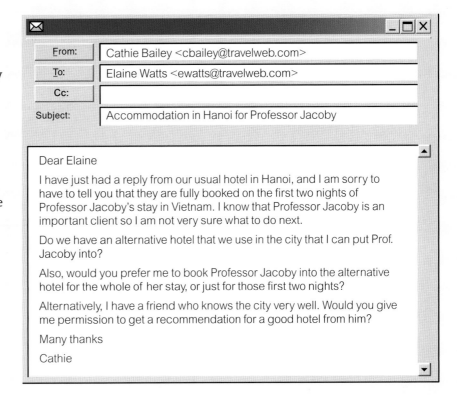

From: Cathie Bailey <cbailey@travelweb.com>

To: Elaine Watts <ewatts@travelweb.com>

Cc:

Subject: Accommodation in Hanoi for Professor Jacoby

Dear Elaine

I have just had a reply from our usual hotel in Hanoi, and I am sorry to have to tell you that they are fully booked on the first two nights of Professor Jacoby's stay in Vietnam. I know that Professor Jacoby is an important client so I am not very sure what to do next.

Do we have an alternative hotel that we use in the city that I can put Prof. Jacoby into?

Also, would you prefer me to book Professor Jacoby into the alternative hotel for the whole of her stay, or just for those first two nights?

Alternatively, I have a friend who knows the city very well. Would you give me permission to get a recommendation for a good hotel from him?

Many thanks

Cathie

5 Email to a colleague at work

Cathie wrote to her friend who works in another travel agency.

1 Read Cathie's email. How can you tell that Russell is a friend and not a superior?

2 Imagine you are Russell. Write back to Cathie and recommend the Lucky Plaza Hotel. Choose four or five pieces of information from the web page to describe the key features of the hotel.

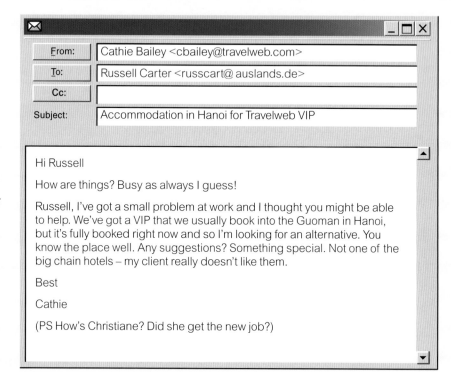

From:	Cathie Bailey <cbailey@travelweb.com>
To:	Russell Carter <russcart@ auslands.de>
Cc:	
Subject:	Accommodation in Hanoi for Travelweb VIP

Hi Russell

How are things? Busy as always I guess!

Russell, I've got a small problem at work and I thought you might be able to help. We've got a VIP that we usually book into the Guoman in Hanoi, but it's fully booked right now and so I'm looking for an alternative. You know the place well. Any suggestions? Something special. Not one of the big chain hotels – my client really doesn't like them.

Best

Cathie

(PS How's Christiane? Did she get the new job?)

Home

More hotels

Excursions

FAQ

Lucky Plaza Hotel ★★☆

HANOI – VIETNAM

Description

* The Lucky Plaza Hotel is located in the centre of Hanoi, in a quiet part of the old quarter.

* Built in 1918, this French colonial-style building has been recently renovated and now offers 50 quiet guest rooms with excellent views over the nearby gardens.

* 50 rooms and suites equipped with AC, satellite TV, in-house movie, IDD phone, mini-bar, music system, and executive desk.

* Deluxe: 38 large, elegant rooms with garden and city view.

* Suite: 12 larger rooms, double view of garden and city view.

Room	Single	Double
Deluxe	US$45	US$55
Suite	US$55	US$65

Restaurants and other services:

* Restaurant: the cafe serves a variety of European, Vietnamese, and Chinese specialities.

* Internet, email service available.

6 Fax

1 Sometimes a fax can be more useful than email. Read the fax and answer the questions.

1 Who is it from and who is it to?

2 Where do these people work?

3 Why do they know each other?

4 Why has a fax been used?

2 You work for Globe Travel in Birmingham. You need to send a map of the location of his hotel to Mr Stuart Hosfield, a client. You are also going to send him a copy of his hotel voucher, and you need him to tell you if he wants a smoking or a non-smoking room in the hotel. Prepare a fax cover sheet. Mr Hosfield's fax and phone numbers are 0121 456 1784 and 0121 456 1766.

FAX COVER SHEET

GLOBE TRAVEL
23, Cotteridge Lane
Birmingham B12 2HX
Tel: 0121-485-1478
Fax: 0121-485-1480

To: Globe Travel, Sheffield Main Office

From: Savita Kumar

Attention of: Anna Hudson

Date: 25 Nov 06

Fax number: 0114 236 2688

Phone number: 0114 236 2689

Total pages, including cover sheet: 4

Comments:

Anna

Here are the three pages of the Edwards brochure that you needed. I tried scanning them to you but it didn't work. There are still some things where good old faxes are better than email!

Will send 2 or 3 full brochures to you asap.

Best

Savita

7 Messages and memos

1 Read these messages.

1 Which one is

a a text message from a mobile phone?

b a typed internal memo?

c a handwritten telephone message?

2 Which one has a problem with

a a fax?

b a delayed train?

c people not checking their emails?

3 Find abbreviations for

a as soon as possible

b concerning / about

c November

d See you

e meeting

f Curriculum Vitae.

2 Write the messages from these notes. Decide if it should be a memo, a phone message, or a text. Make sure you include two of each type.

1 Any ideas for the hotel end-of-season staff party?

2 Ralf can't make lunch today. Text him with an alternative time to meet.

3 Reminder about security – after recent series of thefts from people walking into the travel agency office.

4 Zurich office needs to know when the brochures were sent out – reply before 5 p.m. today.

5 John needs Frank's mobile number immediately.

6 Good luck on your first day in the new job (from Mum).

7 You've left your mobile on the coach. Do you want it brought over to the office?

1

⊕ AT Travel

Memo

From: Peter Halford

To: All staff

Date: 19 Nov 2006

Re: New tours

Just a reminder to you all that we are launching a new range of tours for the 18 to 30 age group next season. Please make sure you are all familiar with the tours, the details of which are attached to the email I sent to all departments last week, but which I don't think some of you have looked at.

Can you also please make sure you check your email regularly?

Peter

2

Telephone message

For: Greg

Time: 10:00 Friday

Johann phoned. Can you call him back asap? It's about the CV you faxed over – he can't read it.

Taken by: Alex

3

Message 1

TRAIN DELAYED.
BE AT MTG 5.
CU. SIMON

Writing bank key

1 Personal statement (p. 52)

1 1 children's entertainer or nanny
2 friendly, hardworking, creative, enjoys working with people, willing to work long hours, tourism training certificate, experience with childcare

2 Letter of application (p. 53)

1 1 children's entertainer or nanny
2 from her Personal Statement: childcare experience, languages
extra: age, current study details

3 Email to a client (p. 54)

1 1 From: Hiromi Murakami
For: Abdhol Kaboodvand
About: Flight details Tokyo to Lima
2 Lima; 14.40 on 20 December
3 send his full name; send his passport number; confirm if he is happy with an electronic ticket

2 Possible answer

Dear Mr Kaboodvand

I have found a flight leaving Lima on the Wednesday at 14.30h. This flight would get you back to Tokyo early the next day. The flight details are:
Return journey (Wed 20th Dec) AA950
Dep: Lima (LIM) 14:30h
Arr: Dallas/Fort Worth (DFW) 20:35h
   JL5013
Dep: Dallas/Fort Worth (DFW) 22:10h
Arr: Tokyo Narita (NRT) 02:40h
Code Share Flight with AA (American Airlines).

I need to confirm this as soon as possible, so could you let me know if this flight is OK for you. I also need to know if you want an electronic ticket or a paper one.

I look forward to hearing from you.

Yours sincerely

4 Email to one of your bosses (p. 55)

1 Dear Elaine
I am sorry to have to tell you that …
would you prefer me to …
Would you give me permission to …
Many thanks

2 Possible answer

Dear Elaine

I have just been talking to Dr Leshem. I am sorry to have to say that he made a mistake with the dates he gave me for a flight I booked for him. I have already issued the ticket, and the conditions do not officially accept changes. I know that Dr Leshem is an important client so I am not very sure what to do.

Technically he should buy a new ticket. However, I have a friend at KLM. Would you give me permission to ring my friend and ask her to help me to change Dr Leshem's ticket?

Many thanks

5 Email to a colleague at work (p. 56)

1 Hi Russell
How are things? Busy as always I guess!
Russell, I've got …
Best

2 Possible answer

Hi Cathy
Good to hear from you. Yes, things are busy. As always! But Cristiane got the job and is very happy. We both are!
For your client, I recommend the three-star Lucky Plaza Hotel. It's located in the centre of Hanoi, in a quiet part of the old quarter. It's an old building in French colonial style so I think your client will like it. It has been recently renovated so it has the usual services like restaurant, Internet, etc.
There are 50 rooms with AC, TV, etc. They all have good views of the nearby gardens. There are also deluxe rooms and suites and these will be best for your client. The deluxe rooms are $55/night, and the suite $65. Not too expensive.
Hope this helps.
Best
Russell
(P.S. When are you coming to see us?)

6 Fax (p. 57)

1 1 From: Savita Kumar. To: Anna Hudson.
2 Globe Travel.
3 Because they work in different branches of the same company.
4 Savita couldn't scan the pages to Anna by email.

2 Possible answer

Dear Mr Hosfield
Here is the map of the location of your hotel and a copy of your hotel voucher. Could you tell me if you want a smoking or a non-smoking room? I need this information to complete the booking.

Yours sincerely
Edward Ho

7 Messages and memos (p. 58)

1 1 a 3   b 1   c 2
2 a 2   b 3   c 1
3 a asap   b Re   c Nov
   d CU   e mtg   f CV

2 Possible answer

1 Memo
From: Jason Masters, manager
To: All staff
Date: 19 Nov 2006
Re: Staff party
As you know we are approaching the end of the season, so it's time to think about the end-of-season staff party. Please let me know if you have any suggestions. Last year we had a great karaoke evening, but perhaps we could do something different this time.

2 (text)
Sorry u can't do lunch. Tmrw 13.00?

3 Memo   AT Travel
From: Peter Halford
To: All staff
Date: 19 Nov 2006
Re: Security
We have had a number of thefts recently from people walking into the office. I would like to remind you all to be extra careful about security. If you see anyone acting suspiciously, please go over and talk to them.

4 Telephone message
For: Peter
Time: 14.00
Zurich office phoned – when were the brochures sent out? Can you call back before 5 p.m.?
Taken by: Alex

5 (phone message, but could be a text)
Telephone message
For: Frank
Time: 14.30
John phoned. He needs your mobile number asap.
Taken by: Alex

6 (text, but could be a phone message)
Good luck! Love Mum xx

7 Telephone message
For: Jenny
Time: 15:00
Coach driver called. You've left your mobile on the coach. Do you want it brought to the office?
Taken by: Alex

7 Accommodation

Take off

1 Make a list of different types of tourist accommodation in your country.

2 Which of these have you stayed in?

3 Tell your partners about the best / worst / most unusual accommodation you have ever stayed in.

Vocabulary

Types of accommodation

1 Match the pictures to the different types of accommodation.

apartment
bed and breakfast
campsite
caravan
chalet
country house
cruise ship
farmhouse
guest house
hostel
hotel
lodge
log cabin
motel
motorhome
mountain refuge
university hall of
  residence
villa

1

2

3

4

5

6

2 Which of these types of accommodation do you have in your country?

3 Think about each type of accommodation. Is it serviced (meals are provided) or self-catering (you cook your own meals)? Discuss this in pairs or groups and complete the diagram. (Hint: Some types will fit into either category. Put these into the shaded area.)

self-catering   serviced

4 Now repeat your discussion, but this time categorize the different types of accommodation as

1 urban *or* rural
2 static *or* mobile.

Make a new diagram for each discussion.

Find out

Go to the Internet or your local tourist information office. Find serviced or self-catering accommodation in your area that would be suitable for

1 a family (two adults, two small children) on holiday, but with a limited budget

2 a business traveller staying in your area for three days for a conference

3 a retired couple who want to see the important monuments in your area

4 a student like you.

Reading

What makes a good hotel?

1 What do people want from a hotel? A good bed? A comfortable room? A modern building? Work in pairs. Make a list of five things you would expect from a good hotel.

2 Look at the hotel web pages. Which hotel
   1 is the best for business travellers?
   2 sounds the most luxurious?
   3 is the most attractive to you?

EL HANA BEACH

Tunisia

Official Rating – 3* – Bed and Breakfast / Half-board

A comfortable, 3-star hotel situated in a garden of palm trees, next to the lovely Sousse beach and within walking distance of the Medina.

Accommodation

Twin and family rooms that can accommodate up to 4 guests. Modern furnishings with bright colours. Air-conditioning, telephone, private bathroom with WC. Balcony with partial sea view.

Facilities and Services

The main restaurant in the hotel serves a large American-style breakfast buffet and dinner buffet. There are 3 indoor bars and a comfortable snack bar.

Radisson SAS Hotel

Nice, France

Discover a new world of sensations at the French Riviera – stay at the landmark Radisson SAS Hotel in Nice where excellence meets originality in a modern ambience.

The hotel features 331 rooms and suites decorated in three imposing and original designs.

With 11 excellent meeting rooms, our hotel can accommodate 400 in the new ballroom and 300 for lunch or dinner on the rooftop terrace.

Ideally located on the famous Promenade des Anglais between the romantic old town and the Arenas Business Park, the Radisson SAS Hotel in Nice is easily accessible by train, plane, and car. The hotel is a five-minute drive from Nice International Airport, and a ten-minute walk from the train station.

Ballymaloe

Cork, Ireland

Ballymaloe is a large country house on a 400-acre farm 20 miles east of Cork City, Ireland. The hotel is family run. Guests enjoy comfortable accommodation and an award-winning restaurant in pleasant rural surroundings.

Ballymaloe is 5 km from several seaside villages that provide fishing, bathing beaches, and beautiful cliff walks. Hotel facilities include an outdoor swimming pool, small golf course, tennis court, woodland walks, and a children's play area. There is often live music in the evening.

Holiday / vacation and small conference venue.

Worldwide capacity of hotels and similar establishments reached an estimated total of 17.4 million rooms in 2001, almost 5 million more than in 1990 (+37%). Expressed in bed-places the capacity is roughly double, as rooms on average count two bed-places.

Vocabulary

Services and facilities

1 Match these facilities and services with the icons.

a   air conditioning
b   baby sitting
c   beauty parlour
d   boutique
e   car park
f   conference facilities
g   safe box
h   direct dial telephone
i   gymnasium
j   hairdryer
k   internet connection
l   jacuzzi
m   laundry service
n   minibar
o   outdoor swimming pool
p   pay TV
q   radio
r   restaurant
s   satellite TV
t   room service
u   wake-up call
v   sauna
w   sea view

2 In your opinion, which are the five most important hotel services and facilities in

1   a hotel for business people and conference delegates?

2   a holiday hotel complex on the coast?

3   a small hotel in the countryside?

3 Explain your choice to your partner.

● Language spot

Describing location

1 Look at these phrases. They say where the El Hana hotel is.

EXAMPLES
in a garden of palm trees
next to the lovely Sousse beach
within walking distance of the Medina

Find similar phrases for the other two hotels.

2 Think of three different hotels in your area. Write a sentence describing the location for each hotel. Call the hotels *Hotel 1*, *Hotel 2*, and *Hotel 3*.

3 Show your partner your descriptions. Do they know which hotels you are describing?

>> Go to **Grammar reference** p.123

Speaking

Giving information about hotels

1 Work in pairs. Student A, you are a travel agent. Look at the information on p.111.

Student B, you are the client. You want a hotel in Tenerife in the Canary Islands. Telephone your travel agent and ask about

1   the location of your hotel
2   hotel restaurants
3   facilities and services for your children
4   car rental
5   night-time entertainment.

2 Now change roles. Student B, you are the travel agent. Look at the information on p.117.

Student A, you are the client. You want a business hotel in Frankfurt, Germany. Telephone your travel agent and ask about

1   the location of your hotel
2   access to the financial district of the city
3   business facilities and services
4   access to the airport
5   restaurants and bars.

profitable (adj) that makes money

pitch (n) a place to put up a tent

seasonality (n) when sth happens at a particular time of year

It's my job

Celina Alvarez Valle

Campsites are the most economical form of accommodation, and are popular wherever the weather is good. But are they the most relaxing places to work? And would you fit in well with a team of campsite workers? Read on and find out.

Celina and her family run a small campsite in the Picos de Europa mountains in northern Spain.

Q Celina, tell us a little bit about how Camping Picos de Europa began.

A Well, originally we were farmers, but in 1989 some friends suggested that a campsite would be a **profitable** business here. Tourism was just becoming popular in the area then.

Q And how many places does the campsite have now?

A Right now it's got 140 **pitches**.

Q How many people is that if the campsite's full?

A Well, you can multiply that by three, or sometimes more. It depends on the time of the year.

Q So with a campsite, there is a certain amount of **seasonality**?

A Yes. Here the season for camping is very short. The best months are May, June, and September. And the really busy months are from mid-July to the end of August.

Q How many people work here in August?

A Ten people, more or less. Sometimes more.

Q And what do they do in general?

A Let's see … cleaning, helping in the

restaurant, reception duties, looking after the shop, and helping in the kitchen, of course. Then there's the swimming pool, which also needs quite careful maintenance. And we need a person to look after the washing machines and dryers, and to clean the washing rooms, the sinks, and the showers.

Q When you decide to employ somebody in the campsite, what do you look for in that person?

A Well, above all honesty. Next they have to be able to get on with people. Campers are very nice people but they are very different one from each other. And you have to know how to work in a team. That's essential. And no bad habits! A non-smoker!

Listening

A place to stay

1 🎧 Listen to these people asking for accommodation.
Which type of accommodation is each speaker looking for?

Speaker	Type	Number / guests	Length of stay	Other details
Richard				
Susan				
Radka				

2 🎧 Listen again. How many people is each enquiry for, and for how long?

3 🎧 If necessary, listen a third time and note any specific details of each call.

budget (adj) very cheap

budget (n) a plan of how to spend an amount of money over a particular period of time

chic (adj) fashionable and elegant

unrivalled (adj) much better than any other of the same type

Reading

Accommodation in Scotland

1 What types of accommodation would you expect to find in Scotland? Make a list with your partner.

2 Read the website for Scotland.

  1 How many different types of accommodation does it offer?

  2 Which type of popular, budget accommodation is not mentioned on the website?

  3 Which are the most unusual types of accommodation mentioned?

  4 Which of the types of accommodation on the web page attracts you most? Why?

| Accommodation | What to do | Special offers | How to get there |

Come to Scotland

Popular locations

Aberdeen Hotels	Glasgow Hotels
Aviemore Hotels	Inverness Hotels
Dundee Hotels	Loch Lomond Hotels
Edinburgh Hotels	Oban Hotels and Bed and Breakfast
Bed and Breakfast Edinburgh	Pitlochry Hotels and Guest Houses
Fort William Hotels	Hotels in St Andrews

Vocabulary

Describing accommodation: adjectives and nouns

1 You can have *a metropolitan hotel* but you cannot have *a metropolitan cottage*. Why not?

2 Match adjectives from A with nouns from B.

A	B
1 five-star	a apartment
2 country	b bed and breakfast
3 converted	c cabin
4 budget	d cottage
5 friendly	e farmhouse
6 metropolitan	f guest house
7 medieval	g hostel
8 modern	h hotel
9 self-catering	i motel
10 stylish	j villa

3 Which adjective can describe most nouns? Which adjectives combine with only one of the nouns?

4 How many meaningful combinations can you make with two adjectives and a noun?

EXAMPLE
There is a huge range of modern, budget hotels in London.

5 Choose different adjective–noun combinations and use them to write sentences to describe accommodation you have stayed in as a tourist.

A Warm Welcome Guaranteed

Scotland's **unrivalled** range of holiday experiences is matched only by the variety of quality accommodation on offer. Whether for a short break or a longer stay, you'll be able to choose from **chic** metropolitan hotels and stylish country houses to friendly bed and breakfasts and comfortable self-catering apartments. Search our wide range of accommodation in Scotland to plan your perfect trip. And for something just a little out of the ordinary – perhaps a converted church, a former lighthouse, or even a medieval castle, there are plenty of opportunities available to fire your imagination. Alternatively search our unrivalled array of self-catering in Scotland. Whatever your **budget** or itinerary, you can find your ideal place to stay using the online accommodation search facility or by getting in touch with our contact centre. All establishments have been inspected under the Visit Scotland Quality Assurance scheme and of course, a warm welcome and true Scottish hospitality come as standard.

restored (adj) put back into its former condition

steeped in (adj) having a lot of, full of sth

surroundings (n) everything that is near or around you

sleeping bag (n) a large soft bag that you use for sleeping in when you go camping, etc.

Mammut Snow Hotel
Type: Ice / Igloo
Location: Finland

Mammut Snow Hotel with its arctic **surroundings** is a unique place. It is an excellent way to experience the coldness of an arctic night. The temperature in the hotel rooms is approximately -5°C, but guests will have a good night's sleep in a warm Ajungilak **sleeping bag**. In Mammut Snow Hotel there are 30 double rooms, 2 group rooms for five persons, and a suite.

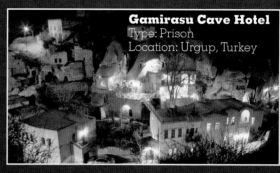

Gamirasu Cave Hotel
Type: Prison
Location: Urgup, Turkey

Gamirasu is the name of an exquisitely **restored** eighteen-room cave house, in Ayvali Village near Urgup in the heart of Cappadocia, Turkey. In former times housing the cells of a prison, this ancient monastery is **steeped** in history. A luxurious cave accommodation in a traditional Cappadocian village.

Speaking

Unusual accommodation

Hotels, guest houses, villas, and campsites are all standard types of accommodation. But what about the unusual?

1 Look at the hotel descriptions . Which hotel is the most unusual?

2 Which hotel would you like to stay in? Why?

3 If you can, go to the websites for the hotels and find out more about them.

4 Work with a partner. Think about your local area. Discuss buildings or natural structures (e.g. caves) that you could convert into 'unusual' accommodation. You might like to consider the following points:

- type – details of type + natural or made structure
- location – urban or rural
- serviced or self-catering
- luxury or budget
- large or small (number of rooms – how many doubles, singles, etc.)
- details of the rooms, facilities, and services.

5 Present your unusual hotel to the rest of the class. You can start like this.

EXAMPLE
We have decided to make our unusual accommodation from [name of structure]. This is a natural / built structure in an urban / rural setting.
We are going to make serviced / self-catering accommodation and it's going to be …

Writing

Local accommodation

Write an introduction to tourist accommodation in your area. You will need to include information about

- the different types of accommodation
- typical accommodation in (a) urban areas and (b) rural areas
- types of accommodation that are typical of your country
- accommodation for people (a) on holiday and (b) on business
- one example of 'unusual' accommodation if you can find one (if there is no unusual accommodation in your area, include your idea from the *Speaking* activity)
- where you can get more information (websites, etc.).

Listening

Taking a reservation by telephone

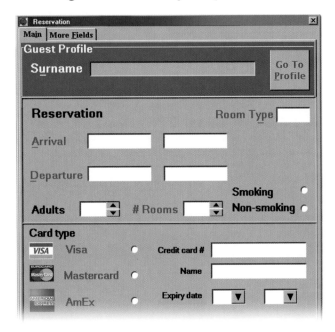

1 🎧 Look at the screen from a hotel computer reservation system. In which order do you think the receptionist will ask for the information? Listen to a phone call and see if you were right.

2 🎧 Listen again and fill in the missing information.

Pronunciation

1 🎧 Listen to the receptionist again. In each question or phrase, underline the word that is stressed most.

1 Can I help you?
2 Would that be a single room?
3 Would you prefer a twin …
4 … or two singles?

In phrases of spoken English we stress one word more than the others. This word represents the most important idea we want the listener to focus on.

2 Look at the following questions from the telephone reservation. Which word will be stressed most in each?

1 What name is it, please?
2 Could you spell that, please?
3 Could you give me the number of the card?
4 Is that Visa, Ms Steinmetz?
5 Could you just tell me the expiry date?

3 Practise saying these questions with the stress on the right word.

Customer care

Smile on the phone

SMILE AND THE WORLD SMILES WITH YOU!

Taking routine phone calls can be boring, but often a phone call is the first contact a guest has with a hotel, and gives a first impression. So smile as you take the booking. The caller will notice the smile in your voice and respond accordingly.
Hotel Training Manual

Try this experiment. Work with a partner. Stand back to back. Take turns to say one of the sentences in the *Pronunciation* section above. Smile when you say some of the sentences. Can your partner 'hear the smile' in your voice?

Speaking

Taking a telephone booking

1 Work in pairs. Student A, you are the receptionist at the Hadrian Hotel. Answer the phone and follow the telephone booking sequence. Take notes of the booking details.

State name of hotel. State own name. Greet client.

⬇

Determine client's room needs – dates, number of guest(s), number of rooms, room type(s)

⬇

Double check dates and needs

⬇

Check availability

⬇

Take client's name

⬇

Request confirmation (fax, email, or credit card)

⬇

Double check details of the confirmation option taken

⬇

Give client reservation number and request its use for booking changes

⬇

Close conversation

Student B, you are the caller. Use the information on p.111.

2 Now change roles.

3 Make up your own caller and accommodation information. You do not need to limit yourselves to hotels. Phone each other and book accommodation.

Checklist

Assess your progress in this unit. Tick (✓) the statements which are true.

I can organize tourist accommodation into different categories

I can understand texts describing tourist accommodation

I can understand people asking about different types of accommodation

I can describe the location, services, and facilities of a hotel

I can take a hotel room reservation by telephone

Key words

Nouns

apartment	hostel
bed and breakfast	meeting room
campsite	refuge
conference facilities	room service
cottage	sea view
country house	suite
direct dial telephone	wake-up call
guest house	

Adjectives

air-conditioned
budget
en-suite (facilities)
five-star
metropolitan
self-catering
serviced

Next stop

1 Where are holidays advertised in your country, and at what time of the year?

2 What sort of holidays are advertised most on TV?

3 Has a magazine or TV advertisement for a holiday destination ever been the reason for you to go there?

8 Marketing and promotion

Take off

1 Make a list of five different products from the tourism industry.

EXAMPLE *a package holiday*

2 Think of different ways you could advertise them. Which ones are the most effective?

The marketing process in travel and tourism

Every day of our lives we can see examples of travel and tourism marketing around us – adverts on TV, adverts in newspapers and magazines, brochures in travel agencies, internet pages, posters in stations, etc. This is because all tourism businesses need to market their products if they hope to be successful. But marketing is not just advertising; it is about researching and identifying the needs of a specific group of customers, and then creating a product that satisfies them.

A large hotel chain, for example, will spend a lot of time and money finding out what its guests want – what kind of services and facilities they need most, which location they prefer, or how much they are prepared to pay. It will then develop a new product, taking care to gear it to the customers' needs. Then, once the company has the right product, it will use different promotional techniques to let its clients know about it.

Private companies are not the only ones that use marketing. Tourist boards and other public sector organizations also have products, and it is important that their customers are aware that these exist. From a museum in a country village to the multiple attractions of a major city like Sydney, all travel and tourism products need good marketing.

Reading
What is marketing?

1 Look at the statements on marketing. Decide if they are true or false.
1 Marketing is the same as advertising.
2 Marketing means knowing what your customers want.
3 Marketing is what you do before the product is sold.
4 Marketing is done by both public and private organizations.

2 Now read about the marketing process and find out if you were right.

3 Which stage are these marketing activities part of
1 develop?
2 monitor?
3 research?

4 Which stage of marketing
1 is the most expensive?
2 needs most creativity?

5 Which part of the marketing process do you think you would be good at? Why?

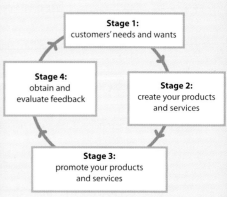

The Marketing Process

Stage 1: customers' needs and wants

Stage 2: create your products and services

Stage 3: promote your products and services

Stage 4: obtain and evaluate feedback

The marketing process does not end after a product has been sold, however. Customers might not be happy with it, and of course people's tastes change with time. Because of this, it is essential to evaluate how customers feel about a product. With the results of the evaluation, it is then possible to improve your product, and in this way continue to meet your customers' expectations.

Vocabulary

Marketing terminology

Match 1–9 with a–i to produce nine marketing tips.

1 (M)onitor …   a   and wants are the first thing you must find out.

2 (A)dvertise …   b   your customers' preferences by using market research.

3 (R)esearch …   c   the effectiveness of your advertising and promotional techniques.

4 (K)nowledge …   d   uses questionnaires to find out what people want.

5 (E)valuate …   e   of what your clients want is essential in marketing.

6 (T)astes …   f   the market carefully before you create your product.

7 (I)dentify …   g   your product in the places where your customers will see it.

8 (N)eeds …   h   your product towards your clients.

9 (G)ear …   i   change with time so products must change too.

● Language spot

Verb patterns

1 Look at this phrase using the verb *gear*.

to gear it to the customer's needs

Now look at the dictionary entry for the verb *gear*.

> **gear** verb
> PHRASAL VERBS gear sth to / towards sb / sth (often passive) to make sth suitable for a particular purpose or person: *There is a special course geared towards the older learner.*

2 What do you think *sb* and *sth* mean?

3 Now look at these other verb phrases from the article on marketing.

1 … if they *hope* to make a profit.
2 … to *let* its clients know about it.

Which verb patterns do they use? Choose from the following

a   hope to do sth   c   let sb / sth do sth
b   hope sth to sb / sth   d   let sb / sth to do sth

4 Complete the sentences using *gear*, *hope*, or *let*.

1   We _____ to have the new product on the market next year.

2   We've decided to _____ the hotel to business tourism.

3   They _____ to increase their profits by using promotional techniques.

4   If you _____ experts do your marketing, you will get better results.

5   A questionnaire in each room _____ guests make comments on the room.

6   Tourism providers have to _____ their products to what the customer wants.

>> Go to **Grammar reference** p.124

Customer care

Learn from your customers

Learn from your customers

Ask for feedback from your customers. Use a questionnaire – keep it short and simple. Get customers to suggest how you could improve your services or even discover what you are particularly good at.

What areas would you want to find out about in a feedback questionnaire

a hotel?   a travel agent?   an airline?

array (n) a large collection of things, especially one that is impressive and is seen by other people

grain (n) the seeds of wheat, rice, etc.

tilt (v) to move, or make sth move, into a position with one end or side higher than the other

warehouse (n) a building where large quantities of goods are stored before being sent to shops

Where in the world?

1   Look at the photos of Newcastle and Gateshead. What sort of cities are they? What sort of tourism will they attract? What sort of things will tourists be able to do there?

2   Read about tourism in NewcastleGateshead. As you read, link the names in the text to the photos.

3   Which three attractions appeal to you most?

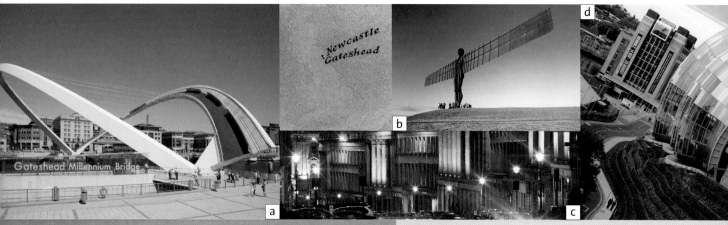

Gateshead Millennium Bridge

NewcastleGateshead's Tourist Top 10

Here is an ultimate list of the top 10 'must see' sights in NewcastleGateshead (in no particular order!), to make sure you get the most out of a visit to the city.

1 Newcastle Quayside and Gateshead Quays – some of the city's most contemporary and stylish cultural and leisure attractions can be found along the River Tyne. You shouldn't miss the curved building of the Sage Gateshead music centre designed by the architect Sir Norman Foster.

2 Gateshead Millennium Bridge – the world's first **tilting** bridge situated on the banks of the River Tyne, linking Newcastle Quayside and Gateshead Quays.

3 Newcastle Castle Keep – the site of the 'New Castle' built in 1080 which gave the city its name and was

founded by Robert Curthose, eldest son of William the Conqueror.

4 The Biscuit Factory – the biggest commercial arts space in Europe based in a beautifully restored Victorian building that was once a biscuit factory.

5 The Angel of the North – a multi-award-winning sculpture created by artist Antony Gormley. Standing 20 m high, it is seen by more than 33 million people every year.

6 Grey Street – in the heart of Newcastle's historic Grainger Town and voted the Best Street in Britain by listeners of national station Radio 4.

7 BALTIC Centre for Contemporary Art – one of Europe's largest centres for contemporary art. An art factory based in a converted 1950s **grain warehouse** on Gateshead Quays. Entry is free.

8 Centre for Life – a wildly exciting visitor attraction for all the family. Discover just how truly extraordinary life is – meet your four-billion-year-old family, explore what makes us all different, and test your brainpower.

9 MetroCentre, Gateshead – once again the largest indoor shopping centre in Europe following completion of the new Red Mall. MetroCentre offers a huge array of department stores and speciality shops – all under one roof.

10 Laing Art Gallery – renowned for its stunning **array** of watercolours, costume, silver, glass, pottery, and sculpture and home to major works by leading pre-Raphaelite artists. The gallery also hosts stunning touring exhibitions in the newly refurbished gallery space.

Listening

Analysing your product

1 A SWOT analysis is a basic technique in marketing. The 'S' means 'Strengths'. Do you know what the other three letters mean?

2 🎧 Jean Stewart is the Leisure Product Manager for the NewcastleGateshead Initiative. Listen to her talking about NewcastleGateshead. In what order does she discuss each of the four aspects of the SWOT analysis?

3 🎧 Listen again and tick (✓) the features that she mentions in the table below.

S
1 the local people ☐
2 the beauty of the surrounding countryside ☐
3 the quality of the local food ☐
4 the combination of old and new attractions ☐

O
1 the opening of the Gateshead Sage ☐
2 the perception people have of the North-east ☐
3 the increasing number of flights to and from Newcastle airport ☐

W
1 other UK cities with a similar product ☐
2 poor communications with London ☐
3 the quality of the hotel bedrooms ☐
4 the shortage of hotel bedrooms ☐

T
1 Bristol, Birmingham, and Manchester ☐
2 the perception people have of the North-east ☐
3 the contamination in the River Tyne ☐

Speaking

Do you SWOT?

1 What sort of strengths and weaknesses, opportunities and threats do cities have? Make a list.

2 Work with a partner. Student A, look at p.111. Student B, look at p.116.

Ask your partner about different characteristics of his / her city destination. Put each answer in the appropriate part of your SWOT chart. Ask about

- transport and access
- accommodation
- restaurants, etc.
- local food
- nightlife and clubbing
- museums and art galleries
- activities for families
- the weather
- marketing potential
- marketing strategy
- current advertising
- the image of the city.

Take turns to ask questions. The winner is the first person to identify more than three weaknesses or three threats in their partner's destination.

EXAMPLE
A *Is the local food one of your strengths?*
B *Yes, it is. Our local food is world famous. People come here especially to try the food.*

OR

B *No, it isn't. It's one of our weaknesses, I'm afraid. It's not easy to find local food in our restaurants.*

OR

B *No, it isn't. In fact, it's one of our opportunities. The food here is very good, but it's not very well known.*

3 Think of a city you know well and decide what you think its strengths, weaknesses, opportunities, and threats are. Tell your partner about the city. Can they guess which city it is?

Personal selling is the oldest and most widely used method of creating demand for a product. In the USA over **13 million people** work in sales compared to only 500,000 in advertising.

Listening

Promotion in tourism

1 Look at the diagram about marketing and promotion. Do you understand any of the terms? Can you fill in any of the gaps?

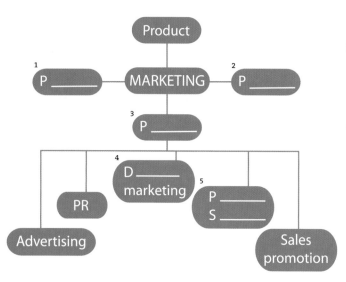

2 🎧 Listen to Jean Stewart talking about promotion and complete the diagram.

3 🎧 Which of the following ideas about promotion does Jean mention directly?

1 To create a demand for a product
2 To explain why a product is better than a competitor's product
3 To make customers aware of a product
4 To remind customers about an existing product

4 🎧 Listen again. Write T (true) or F (false).

1 The marketing mix is made up of product, place, and promotion.
2 Promotion and advertising are the same.
3 Small operators use email for direct marketing.
4 Personal selling is about going from house to house knocking on doors.

Find out

1 How is tourism promoted in your local area?

1 By a government organization like the NewcastleGateshead Initiative
2 By the private sector – Chamber of Commerce, local tourism associations, etc.
3 By both

2 What promotional techniques do your local tourism authorities normally use?

Pronunciation

1 Match the words on the left with their pronunciation transcriptions on the right.

Word		Pronunciation transcription	
1	advertise	a	ˈɪnəvətɪv
2	ancient	b	aɪˈdentɪfaɪ
3	campaign	c	ˈwiːknəsɪz
4	identify	d	ˈædvətaɪz
5	improve	e	streŋθs
6	innovative	f	ˈeɪnʃənt
7	marketing	g	ˈmɑːkɪtɪŋ
8	picturesque	h	pɪktʃəˈresk
9	strengths	i	θrets
10	threats	j	kæmˈpeɪn
11	weaknesses	k	ɪmˈpruːv

2 Which word looks most / least like its transcription?

3 Look at the transcriptions and try pronouncing the words. Let your partner listen to you. Now you listen to your partner.

4 🎧 Listen to the words. How well did you pronounce them?

5 🎧 Listen and repeat each word. Which do you find easiest / hardest to pronounce well?

In 2004 hotels in the USA spent anything between $416 and $4,464 per room on marketing themselves.

Vocabulary

The language of advertising

1 Match the slogans with the pictures.

1 A green Mediterranean haven
2 Unforgettable Cruises
3 Kyrgyzstan – Breathtaking Natural Beauty
4 Mystical Silk Road Tour

2 What does the word *nice* mean? How do you translate it into your language?

3 Substitute the adjectives in the adverts with the word 'nice'. What is the effect?

4 Look at adjectives 1 – 7. For each adjective, find two 'publicity'-style adjectives from a – n.

1	beautiful	a	ancient	h	innovative
2	big	b	diminutive	i	large
3	cheap	c	economical	j	low-cost
4	expensive	d	enormous	k	luxury
5	new	e	exclusive	l	modern
6	old	f	gorgeous	m	picturesque
7	small	g	historic	n	tiny

5 Choose the best adjective for these advertising texts.

1 The region has a lot of *exclusive / historic / picturesque* monuments.

2 Europe's best and biggest *economical / low-cost / modern* airline.

3 The new bridge is one of the most *innovative / modern / picturesque* pieces of engineering in the country.

4 Make yourself feel really special – take a short break in one of our *economical / exclusive / modern* country hotels.

5 Go online and search for what your family needs from our database of hundreds of *enormous / economical / tiny* campsites in Europe.

6 *Diminuitive / Gorgeous / Large* beaches, luxury accommodation, …

6 Choose the two adjectives that you like the most and use them to write tourism slogans for your country.

Writing

Adverts

How would you promote tourism in the area where you live (or any other area you like and know well)?

1 Make a list of the different aspects of the region that make it attractive to tourists.

2 Prepare a web page advertising the region. It will need images as well as text. Which images can you use?

3 If you can, make a 'mock-up' of how you would like your web page to appear in real life.

fragrance (n) a pleasant smell

hold (v) to organize an event

press release (n) an official statement made to journalists by a large organization, a political party, or a government department

scent (n) 1 a pleasant smell 2 a liquid with a pleasant smell that you wear on your skin to make it smell nice

Reading

Promotional techniques

1 Look at these different sales promotion techniques.

- adverts in the media
- brochures and leaflets
- competitions
- discount coupons (in newspapers, etc.)
- discounted prices
- displays and exhibitions
- give-aways (free gifts)
- lotteries and prize draws
- posters
- reports in the media
- websites

Which techniques are used in the four activities below? Are there any other activities in the four campaigns?

2 Judge each activity in terms of cost (C), logistics (L), impact (I), and originality (O). Award each activity a score from 1 (very poor) to 10 (excellent).

		C	L	I	O	Total
1	North-east England					
2	Hong Kong					
3	Rio de Janeiro					
4	Languedoc					

3 Add up the scores for each campaign from the scores for the whole class. Which was the best campaign in each category? Which was the best campaign overall?

North-east England

The Days Out Campaign was launched in July and was aimed at enticing people to get out and about within the region, visiting both paying and non-paying attractions.

The campaign got a 'flying start' with 500 balloons released from Durham Cathedral on Monday 19 July 2004. The lucky person finding the balloon which had travelled the furthest was rewarded with a free day out visiting some of the region's best attractions.

Hong Kong

The Hong Kong Tourism Board announced a new tourism promotion plan on Sunday .

Selina Chow Liang Shuk-Yee, chairwoman of Hong Kong Tourism Board, said in a **press release** on Sunday that Hong Kong is to launch a two-month 'hospitality month', during which discounted air tickets and hotel charges will be offered to tourists.

Rio de Janeiro

Indians from Brazil's Amazon region painted an Indian logo on visitors' arms at the Brazilian International Tourism Promotional Campaign **held** in Rio de Janeiro, Brazil, 26 May, 2004. The tourism promotional campaign attracted several hundred people from more than 40 countries.

Languedoc

The Languedoc Regional Committee ran a campaign to draw people's attention to the Languedoc's sunny, wide-open spaces. An American company, Prolitec, suggested giving the message more impact by using outdoor smells. Prolitec created a **fragrance** that would remind people of the typical regional **scent** of brush land. The scent was then used in a seven-day advertising campaign run in winter in major train stations in Paris and the south of France.

● Language spot

Superlatives

1 Use the words in brackets to complete these statements.

1 The Brazilian campaign was the _____ (cheap).

2 The Languedoc campaign had the _____ (high) impact.

3 The _____ (original) campaign was the one by the Languedoc Regional Committee.

2 Look at the results in your table for the four campaigns. Make sentences to describe what your group voted.

≫ Go to **Grammar reference** p.124

Speaking

Presenting a campaign

1 Work in groups of three or four. Design a campaign for a tourism area you know well. Think about the four factors that make a good campaign.

2 Present your campaign. Award marks for the campaigns of other groups.

Writing

Promotional campaign news

1 Write a news item for a web page or a travel magazine describing your campaign. Use the web pages from *Reading* to help you. Think about how you can illustrate the page, and about which links you would put to other useful web pages.

2 Make a 'mock-up' of your page as you would like it to appear in real life. Better still, if you can, upload your page on to a suitable server and invite colleagues and friends to visit it.

Checklist

Assess your progress in this unit. Tick (✓) the statements which are true.

I can read and understand simple articles about marketing

I can understand people talking about marketing and promotion

I can use a range of adjectives to write simple advertising texts

I can make a presentation of a promotional campaign

I can write a press release describing a promotional campaign

Key words

Nouns

campaign	strength
expectation	threat
marketing	weakness
opportunity	

Adjectives

ancient	picturesque
enormous	promotional
innovative	tiny
luxury	

Verbs

advertise
develop
evaluate
identify
improve
market
monitor
research

Next stop

1 How many different airlines can you name?

2 Which of these are 'low-cost' airlines?

3 Tell your partner about the last place you went to by plane. (If you haven't flown yet, tell your partner about the place you would like to go.)

9 The airline industry

Take off

1 Match the words and phrases from the list with the pictures about flying.

boarding card	landing	take-off
check-in	passenger cabin crew	taxi
cruise	security control	

2 Number the pictures in the right order for a typical flight.

3 🎧 Listen and check.

Listening

The ups and downs of flying

1 🎧 Four people are discussing how they feel about air travel. Listen and mark what they like with a tick (✔), and what they don't like with a cross (✗). If they don't mind, write **–**.

	Isabel	Alexi	Millie	Gustavo
Travelling to and from airports				
Checking in				
Going through security				
Waiting to embark				
Boarding when you haven't got a seat number				
Taking off				
A window seat				
Landing				
Waiting for your luggage				
Travel delays				

2 Check your answers with your partner, and then listen again if you need to.

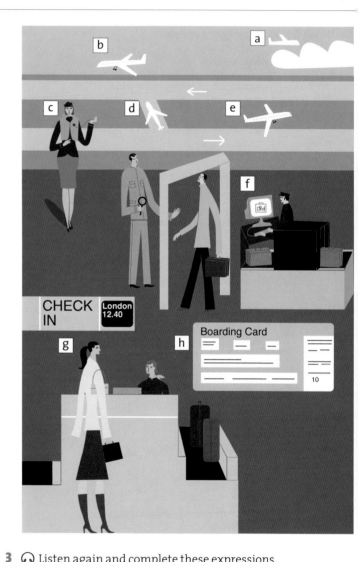

3 🎧 Listen again and complete these expressions.

1 I actually _____ _____ to the airport …

2 And I _____ _____ landing.

3 I _____ _____ taking off.

4 … and then just rising in the air suddenly. I _____ _____ _____ .

5 I _____ the delays.

6 … being in the airport all day. I _____ _____ that.

7 I _____ _____ waiting to embark.

8 I _____ _____ for luggage.

In this unit
- expressing degrees of like / dislike
- developments in the airline industry
- flying, traditional airlines, and low-cost airlines
- preparing and carrying out customer surveys

● Language spot
'like' or 'dislike'

1 Put the different expressions of 'liking' in order from the most positive to most negative.

don't like	quite like
don't mind	really don't like
hate	really hate
like	really love
love	

2 We can say *I like* … or *I quite like* …, and we can also say *I really like*. What is the difference?

3 Now ask your partners how they feel about each stage of flying, especially
- getting to and from the airport
- queuing at the check-in desk
- going through security control
- waiting in the departure lounge
- taking off
- being in the air
- landing.

>> Go to **Grammar reference** p.124

Vocabulary
Air travel

1 *Fly, flight, flying* – use the correct word to complete each sentence.

1 The first powered _____ was made by the Wright Brothers in 1903.

2 Even though _____ is the safest form of transport, some people are afraid of it.

3 Modern jet aircraft _____ at an altitude of 8,000 to 9,000 metres.

2 What is the difference between the three words?

3 Complete the sentences with a word from the list.

arrivals	depart
arrive	departure
board	land
boarding	landing
check in	take off
check-in	take-off

1 The last time I flew, our _____ was delayed by over two hours.

2 Most airports give information about departures and _____ on TV monitors placed around the airport.

3 When you _____ , the clerk asks you if you have packed your bag yourself.

4 You cannot use electronic equipment during either _____ or landing.

5 Modern navigation systems mean that aircraft can _____ safely at night, in bad weather, and even without a pilot.

6 Even if you have a _____ card, some airlines ask to see your passport as well.

4 Write sentences like this for three of the other words in the list. Ask your partner to complete the sentences.

Air transport

This provides 28 million direct, indirect, and induced jobs worldwide, a figure that is expected to rise to 31 million by 2010.

The accident rate for air travel represents one fatality per million flights. Despite the rapid and constant growth in air traffic, accident rates have been reduced by over 50% during the past twenty years.

Today's aircraft are 70% more fuel-efficient than the jets of the 1960s. Long-term goals include achieving a 50% cut in CO_2 emissions per passenger kilometre for aircraft entering service in 2020.

Reading

Tourism and air travel

1 Look at the title of the article. What do you think the article will be about? Choose from the following possibilities.

   1 The future of air travel
   2 The advantages and disadvantages of air travel
   3 The incredible places you can fly to if you have enough money
   4 How to get the cheapest tickets for different flights

2 Read the article and see if you were right.

3 How many million

   a people travelled by plane in 2005?
   b passengers used Atlanta airport in 2005?
   c people are employed by the airline industry?

4 Find

   1 two advantages of air travel
   2 three disadvantages of air travel.

Find out

1 What is a *carbon offset scheme*? How does it work? (Hint – type 'carbon offset scheme' into an internet search engine like Google.)

2 Which air carriers are currently on the US and EU blacklists?

Pronunciation

1 Look at the names and codes of these airports. How many do you recognise?

Country	Airport name	Airport code
Australia	Delta Downs	DDN
Indonesia	Datadawai	DTD
Pakistan	Dadu	DDU
Taiwan	Taitung	TTT
Tanzania	Tanga	TGT
Tongo	Kuini	NTT
Vietnam	Da Nang	DAD

Fly the world
(but at what price?)

THE DEVELOPMENT OF JET AIRCRAFT HAS REVOLUTIONIZED TRAVEL, making it possible to go much further much faster. New York in the morning. A meeting and lunch in San Francisco. Then back east to Boston, before ending the day in Washington. Almost anything is possible.

And the airline industry is not just fast. It is big. Very big! In fact it's huge, starting with more than three million people employed by the world's airlines, or with the 14,000 airports that passengers fly to or from. How many passengers? Over 1.5 billion worldwide in 2005, with Atlanta International, the world's busiest airport, handling over 80 million passengers alone.

In order to try to keep such a complex industry under control, each of the world's airports has a special code. The International Air Transport Association (IATA) takes responsibility for the designation of these codes , and they can easily be found on the Internet. Every single flight that takes off is also identified by a unique number, called a flight number. This is composed of the airline's code and then three or four digits.

Airlines work through scheduled flights, which take off and land at regular published times, or charter flights that are contracted to fly at a set time. Flights can be short-haul, medium-haul, or long-haul, depending on the distance covered, but whatever the distance, passenger safety is at the heart of all operations, making air travel the safest form of transport by far.

Inevitably air travel creates problems, beginning with some people's fear of flying. More recently, however, the skies we fly have begun to look darker than the industry wants to admit. Security is now a major problem, especially after the devastating impact of the September 11 terrorist attacks on New York and Washington.

Also blackening the skies are the emissions from jet aircraft. A return transatlantic flight, for example, can produce up to two tons of carbon dioxide per passenger! So serious is the problem that in 2005 the UK Environment Minister asked travellers to consider subscribing to one of the carbon offset schemes available. 'It's relatively cheap. For example, the climate change impact of a flight to the Mediterranean only costs around £5 to offset.'

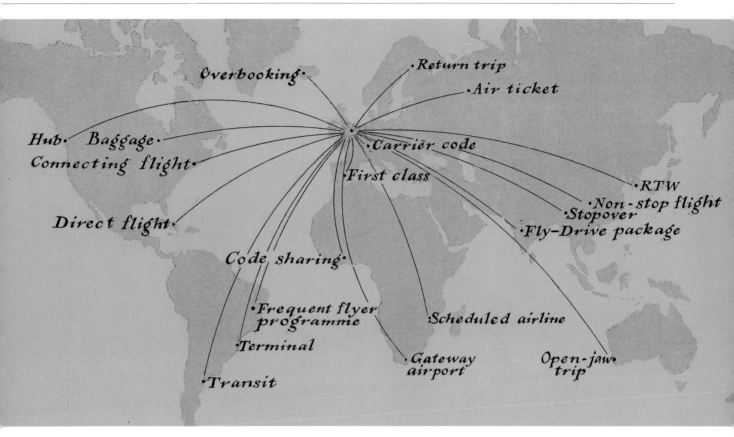

Overbooking·
·Return trip
·Air ticket
Hub· Baggage·
·Carrier code
Connecting flight·
·First class
·RTW
·Non-stop flight
·Stopover
Direct flight·
·Fly-Drive package
Code sharing·
·Frequent flyer
programme
Scheduled airline
·Terminal
·Gateway
airport
Open-jaw·
trip
·Transit

2 🎧 Listen and repeat the pronunciation of the airport codes. Pay special attention to the pronunciation of *t* and *d*.

3 Work with a partner. Ask and answer about airport codes.

EXAMPLE
A *What's the code for Da Nang?*
B *It's DAD.*

4 Say the following words. Pay special attention to *d* and *t*.

boarding card	take off	code
ticket	flight	transit
airport	scheduled	transport
depart		

Speaking
The air travel route map

1 Look at the route map for Bristish Airways. Do you know the names of the countries that correspond to each air travel term? Ask and answer with your partner.

EXAMPLE
A *Which country corresponds to Open-jaw trip?*
B *Australia.*

2 How many terms do you recognize? Work in teams. Team A, look at p.112. Team B, look at p.117. Choose a term and read the definition to the other team. They must guess which term corresponds to the definition they hear.

Take turns to read a definition. The first team with ten correct guesses wins.

3 Work in pairs. Choose a term. Tell your partner the term. Your partner must try to explain the term in her / his own words.

compete (v) to try to win, or achieve sth, or to try to be better than sb else

no-frills (adj) without extra comforts, such as meals, films, etc.

Listening

Low-cost or traditional?

1 Think about the disadvantages of flying with low-cost airlines. In your opinion, what could traditional airlines do to attract customers back? Exchange your ideas with a partner.

2 🎧 Listen to Martin Stanton of the Birmingham College of Food, Tourism, and Creative Studies talking about the advantages and disadvantages of both types of airline. Tick (✓) the characteristics he mentions for each.

Characteristic	Traditional airlines	Low-cost airlines
1 Booking is possible through a travel agent		
2 Booking is easy through the Internet		
3 You can check luggage through to the final destination		
4 You have a seat number before you board		
5 You have the option of different classes of seat		
6 You can go on the plane first with small children		
7 The cabin staff are more friendly		
8 There is more legroom during the flight		

3 Which type of airline is best for people like Martin in your opinion? Why?

4 Which type of airline do you prefer?

Reading

Revolution in the skies

1 Look at the logos on the aircraft tail fins. Which airlines are they from?

2 Are these airlines low-cost (like easyJet) or traditional (like Lufthansa)?

3 Make a list of the reasons for the current success of low-cost airlines. Read the article and see if you were right.

LOW-COST CARRIERS

In the good old days it was easy. Most countries had a national airline: KLM was the Dutch one, LOT the Polish national airline, and so on. The exception to this was the US, where different major airlines such as Pan Am, American Airlines, or Delta, **competed** openly for clients. Most of these airlines offered similar products at more or less the same prices. Of course, some companies concentrated more on short-haul, domestic flights – the sort of flight where you are only just in the air when the cabin crew are telling you to get ready for landing. Others like Qantas became famous for their long-haul, intercontinental routes, offering free stopovers to make eighteen-hour flights more attractive to customers.

The air ticket itself was, and still is, a complex business. The basic return ticket was the commonest: the single ticket was so expensive that nobody ever bought one except in an emergency. And of course, the traditional ticket came in different classes to suit different pockets: economy for the masses, business for the executives, and first class for those lucky few who could pay ten times the economy tariff to get more legroom and a seat that converts into a bed!

The whole system was turned upside down, however, by the arrival of the low-cost carriers. Ryanair got **no-frills** flying going in the early 90s, modelling itself on the American budget airline, Southwest Airlines. easyJet was quick to follow, and since then the idea of getting on a plane the same way you would get on a coach has really taken off, with

4 According to the article, which of the following statements are
  a only true for major airlines?
  b only true for low-cost carriers?
  c true for both types of airline?
  d true for neither type?

  1 They do not have different classes of seating on board their planes.
  2 They offer free in-flight food and entertainment.
  3 They offer free stopovers on long-haul flights.
  4 They often use less important airports.
  5 They only sell single tickets.
  6 They operate long-haul flights.
  7 They operate short- and medium-haul flights.
  8 They spend as little time on the ground as possible.
  9 They use paperless ticketing.

5 Why are low-cost carriers less likely to be interested in long-haul operations?

Germanwings, Smart Wings, BMI Baby, Vueling, and a hundred others. The rest is history, with traditional airlines going deeper and deeper into crisis in this first decade of the new millennium.

The low-cost strategy is based on limited turnaround times at airports – usually twenty to 25 minutes. This means that the airlines can get more flights out of a day – eight as opposed to the normal six. Some low-cost carriers also use secondary airports, with much lower landing and take-off charges. Paperless ticketing and sales over the Internet and the phone also keep costs down. They also issue single tickets only, and of course, there are no first-class or business-class seats. No free newspapers nor free food. In fact, no free anything, although you can pay to buy most things during the flight.

And the future? Paperless ticketing and internet sales from traditional airlines? That's already here. Low-cost flights to long-haul destinations? That's less likely to happen, precisely because of the way low-cost carriers make their money by fitting so many flights into each day. But who knows? The sky's the limit!

Vocabulary

Low-cost carriers

Complete the sentences with terms from the reading.

1 A less technical name for a low-cost carrier is a _____ _____ .

2 A _____ allows you to interrupt a long flight and stay in a city en route to your destination.

3 A _____ - _____ flight is one that does not go further than 1,000 km.

4 _____ - _____ _____ are airlines that offer low fares for basic services with no 'extras' such as meals on the plane.

5 Giving the customer a reference number for a seat on a plane but not a ticket they can hold in their hand is known as _____ _____ .

6 The fees an airline pays to an airport for using its facilities are known as _____ and _____ - _____ _____ .

7 The _____ _____ is the minimum time between a plane landing and taking off.

Writing

Producing a questionnaire

Low-cost carriers have been successful because they asked their clients about their preferences. This kind of research is essential in tourism.

1 Use the notes below to produce a questionnaire for an airline.

2 Ask three or four more questions of your own to complete the survey.

> ★ Age?
> ★ Profession?
> ★ How often/fly?
> ★ Reason – business/leisure?
> ★ Normally use low-cost airlines, or traditional?
> ★ Travel agent/internet bookings – which easier?
> ★ Internet bookings – feel secure sending credit card details, etc.
> ★ Paperless tickets – happy with them?
> ★ Choice of class (business/economy) important?
> ★ Check-in time – 2 hours before flight too long?

● Language spot

Asking questions politely

1 It is very important to ask questions politely when you carry out a survey. It is not a good idea to ask direct questions.

EXAMPLES
How old are you?
What's your job?
Where are you going?

Instead, try to use polite forms.

EXAMPLES
Would you mind telling me how old you are?
Could you tell me what you do?
Can I ask you where you are going?

2 🎧 Listen to the interview with Martin Stanton again, and complete the polite questions.

1 _____ you _____ _____ a couple of questions about air travel?

2 _____ _____ _____ you _____ often you fly?

3 _____ _____ _____ you _____ you use low-cost airlines at all?

3 Now look at *Customer Care*, and then use the advice to interview different people in your class.

>> Go to **Grammar reference** p.124

Customer care

Questionnaire tactics

WE WANT TO KNOW YOU'RE HAPPY!

When you ask a traveller to answer a questionnaire, remember to
● say what the questionnaire is about
● ask permission before you ask any questions
● tell the person how long the interview will last.

It is not enough to ask polite questions. You have to sound polite, too. Smile when you ask your questions. Avoid looking down at your question sheet all the time. Remember to look at the person you are interviewing.
Communication Skills Presentation

1 In which of the pieces of advice would you say
This will only take five minutes.
Excuse me, I'm doing a survey about air travel.
Would you mind answering a few questions?

2 How should you finish a questionnaire? What should you say at the end?

Checklist

Assess your progress in this unit. Tick (✓) the statements which are true.

I can understand people talking about how they feel about air travel

I can discuss my feelings about air travel with colleagues and friends

I can understand articles and news items about the airline industry

I can produce a questionnaire about air travel preferences

I can use indirect questions to be polite when interviewing travellers

It's my job

1 Look at the photo of Javier. Write T (true) or F (false).

1 He's Spanish.
2 He's a pilot.
3 He likes working in tourism.
4 He knows the secret to working in tourism.

2 Now read about Javier and see if you were right.

Javier Díez

Name: Javier Díez

Job: Sales Representative in the flights and reservations section of Aeropostal, the Venezuelan airline

Based: In Madrid

Education: Three years' study at a university college of tourism in Venezuela

Experience: Four years. Started in Venezuela with American Airlines, then moved to Spain to begin in Aeropostal

Future: Become a manager in his present company

Thoughts about:

... his job I like the airline industry. It's what I know, and I like it very much.

... his career I think this career's beautiful – very beautiful and very interesting. We learn so much about the people, about other cultures, but above all, about how to treat the people as we like to be treated.

... tourism In tourism your product is a service. It's not a tangible product, and that's very important. So I think the secret to working in tourism is customer service. You have to be very patient – very, very nice. You have to give the service as you would like to be treated. I think that's the secret – customer service. And as in other areas, you have to like what you're doing and do it well. With love. With care.

Key words

Nouns

air ticket	non-stop flight
baggage	open-jaw trip
boarding card	paperless ticketing
budget airline	return trip
carrier code	scheduled airline
connecting flight	secondary airport
delay	security control
direct flight	stopover
emissions	take-off
low-cost carriers	turnaround time

Adjectives
long-haul (flights)
short-haul (flights)

Next stop

1 What would be a 'normal' holiday for you?

2 Tell your partner about the last 'normal' holiday you had. Where did you go? When? Who with? What did you do?

3 What would be a special holiday for you?

10 Holidays with a difference

Take off

1 What could the two holidaymakers do that is 'different'? Use the pictures at the side to help you.

2 Have you ever had a holiday that was 'different'?

FED-UP WITH THE SAME OLD HOLIDAY?
WHY NOT TRY SOMETHING DIFFERENT?

Listening

At the trade fair

Mariana and Jurgita work for a tour operator. They are visiting a large tourism trade fair in order to gather ideas for an 'alternative tourism' programme. They are thinking about four programmes:

1 'Adventure and action'
2 'Ecotourism and nature'
3 'Escape and enlightenment'
4 'Culture and heritage'.

1 Match the pictures in *Take off* with the categories.

2 Which category would each of these words and places be in?

diving	expedition	gastronomic week
working farm	Mexico	France
volcanoes	biking	cattle ranch
pilgrimage	Antarctica	Costa Rica
white-water rafting	spa and health resorts	horse riding India
ecosystem	the Caribbean	sea-life

3 🎧 Listen to their conversation at the end of the day and check your answers.

4 Which holiday do they choose for each category?

Vocabulary

Different holiday types

1 Put these 'holidays with a difference' into the four categories.
a tour of Scotland visiting historic castles
b mountain climbing
c conservation work helping to repair coastal damage
d windsurfing
e cycling in the mountains and deserts of Mongolia
f four-week trip to Canada to learn English
g trip to Beijing for the 2008 Olympics
h whale-watching off the west coast of the USA
i week at a health farm to relax and 'de-stress'
j long weekend in London to visit museums and art galleries
k learning survival skills in the jungles of Borneo
l pilgrimage to Mecca
m weekend of beauty treatments and relaxation in a country hotel
n off-piste mountain skiing
o weekend break at the Prague Music Festival
p research trip to collect data on ape behaviour in Malaysia

2 Can you do any similar 'alternative holidays' in your country?

3 Match words from A with words from B to make compound nouns for different holiday activities, for example: *sightseeing, mountain climbing*. How many different activities can you list?

A		B	
sight	horse	seeing	climbing
cliff	mountain	boarding	walking
heli	scuba	skiing	watching
snow	water	biking	riding
whale	hang	surfing	diving
hill	wind	rafting	jumping
skate	camel	gliding	
jet	bird		
bungee	white-water		

4 Is it possible to do any of the activities in your city or region?

Reading

The Karakoram Experience

1 Why is the travel company called the *Karakoram Experience*?

2 How many different adventure activities are mentioned or described in the website?

3 What types of scenery and landscape are mentioned?

4 What type of traveller do they try to attract?

KE Adventure Travel

About KE

In 1983 two university friends, Tim Greening and Glenn Rowley, decided to take their passion for travel in Asia and in particular the Karakoram mountains, and create a travel company with a difference: 'The Karakoram Experience'. Today KE Adventure Travel has grown to become one of the world's leading independent specialist travel companies. In addition to our extensive range of worldwide adventures, the staff in our UK and American offices organize tailor-made private expeditions, trips for school groups, and charity treks.

KE ADVENTURES

Peru – in the footsteps of the Incas

Family adventure in the Andes – Horse riding, rafting, biking, and easy trekking – Indian craft market at Pisac – Magical Machu Picchu – Amazon jungle lodge visit

Swedish Lapland – a Winter Wonderland

A winter activity holiday north of the Arctic Circle – Travel by snowmobile and by dogsled – Ski touring and snowshoe hiking – Northern Lights – Fish in a frozen lake – Visit the Icehotel – Meet the Sami people and their reindeer

Costa Rican adventure

Trekking, rafting, and wildlife adventures – Challenging ascent of Volcan Chirripo (3820 m), Costa Rica's highest peak – Rafting on the beautiful Pacuare – Fantastic wildlife – Relaxing on idyllic Pacific Ocean beaches

Listening

Interview with a mountaineer

1 🎧 Listen to an interview with a mountaineer. Answer the questions.

1 How old was he when he did his first climb without his parents?

2 Which of these countries has he been to with a tour company?

Kenya	Peru
Bolivia	Kyrgyzstan
Pakistan	Tajikistan

3 Which of these things does he look for in a tour company?

a cheap price
b a guide for the whole trip
c organisation of local transport, lodging, and permits

4 How high was the highest mountain he's climbed – 6,400 m or 7,400 m?

5 What's the worst moment he's experienced when mountain climbing?

6 What's the happiest moment?

2 🎧 Listen again and complete the questions that the interviewer asks.

1 When _____ you _____ mountain climbing?

2 What _____ expedition mountaineering? When _____ you _____ that?

3 Do you use a _____ _____ when you organize an expedition, or do you _____ _____ _____?

4 How _____ _____ find a suitable company?

5 What _____ you look for in a _____ _____?

6 What's the highest mountain _____ _____?

7 Have you _____ _____ frightened?

8 Have you _____ thought _____ _____ _____?

● Language spot

Asking and talking about experience

Look at these sentences from the interview.
*I've **been** to Central Asia, once to Kyrgyzstan and once to Tajikistan.*
*But both times we **used** a tour company.*

The first sentence is looking at *general* experience with no specific time reference. The second sentence is referring to a *specific* occasion in the past.

1 Which verb is in the Present Perfect and which verb is in the Past Simple?

2 Look at the questions you completed in **2** in *Listening*. Find three examples of the Present Perfect and two examples of the Past Simple.

3 Match questions 1–6 with answers from a–k. There may be more than one possibility.

1	Have you ever been diving?	a	Yes, I did.
2	Did you like it?	b	No, I didn't.
3	Would you like to try it?	c	Yes, it was great.
4	Where did you do it?	d	Not really.
5	Have you thought of trying a windsurfing holiday?	e	Yes, I have.
		f	No, I haven't.
		g	Yes, I would.
6	Would you like some more information?	h	That's a good idea.
		i	Mmm. Tell me more about it.
		j	In Malta.
		k	Yes, please. It sounds interesting.

>> Go to **Grammar reference** p.125

| Ecotourism = responsible travel to natural areas that conserves the environment and sustains the well-being of local people | You can't protect what you don't know.
Lars-Eric Lindblad
Leader of the first commercial Antarctica cruise in 1966 | We should have the sense to leave just one place alone.
Sir Peter Scott
Founder of the World Wildlife Fund |

Speaking

Have you ever ...?

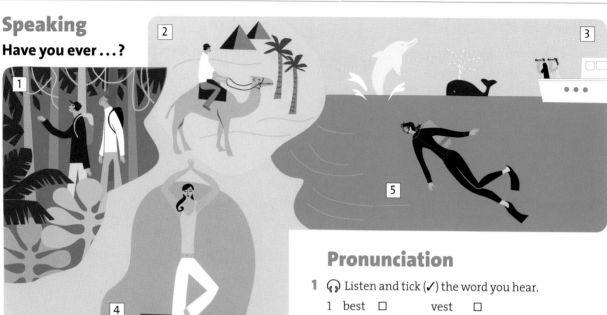

1 Choose one or two of the activities from *Vocabulary: Different holiday types* **3**, and one of the KE Adventure holidays. With a partner, use the information in the following dialogue.

A Have you ever been _____?

B Yes, I have. / No, I haven't.

A Did you like it? / Would you like to try it?

B _____

A Have you thought of trying something different? What about _____?

B That's a good idea. Tell me more about it.

A _____

2 Choose some more activities and adventure holidays. Go round the class and ask different students about their experiences. Tell them about one of the adventure holidays. Try to get them interested in buying it.

3 Report back to your partner on what you found out. How much interest was there in the adventure holidays?

Pronunciation

1 🎧 Listen and tick (✓) the word you hear.

1 best ☐   vest ☐
2 very ☐   berry ☐
3 vine ☐   wine ☐
4 veil ☐   whale ☐
5 best ☐   vest ☐   west ☐
6 bale ☐   veil ☐   whale ☐

2 Practise the words for each sound.

3 Say one of the words from each group in **1**. Your partner will point to the word he / she has heard.

4 Say these words. Think about the pronunciation of b, v, and w.

/b/	/v/	/w/
basic	vacation	wet
Beijing	volcano	white-water
Borneo	activity	wildlife
bungee	diving	worldwide
Caribbean	ever	
rabbits	survival	
scuba	alternative	
	have you ever	
	I've been very busy	

The growth of the adventure tourism market
Growth in adventure holiday market in the last five years = 10–15%
Growth in traditional sun, sea, and sand package holiday market in the last five
years = 4–5%

Where in the world?

Discuss these questions in groups.

1   What do you know about Antarctica – its
    population, its size and location, the number of
    tourists who visit?
2   What type of transport do tourists use to visit
    Antarctica?
3   What activities can tourists do?

Read the text to check your answers.

Speaking

Questions on Antarctica

In pairs, ask each other for information on Antarctic
cruises. Student A, look at p.112. Student B, look at p.117.

Tourism in Antarctica

There are no indigenous people in Antarctica. The population varies
from fewer than 1,000 in winter to almost 20,000 in summer:
5,000 scientists from 27 of the countries belonging to the
Antarctic Treaty, plus 14,000 tourists.

The nearest land mass is South America, which is
approximately 1,000 kilometres from the tip of the
Antarctic Peninsula.

The surface area of Antarctica is 36 million square
kilometres.

Antarctica currently has no economic activity apart from
offshore fishing and tourism, and these are run by other
nations.

Tourism in Antarctica is mainly by around twenty vessels
carrying 45 to 280 passengers each.

Most trips take about ten days to three weeks from port to port.

Antarctic visits are mainly concentrated at ice-free coastal zones over the
Antarctic summer, the five-month period from November to March. In high
summer there will be more than twenty hours of daylight per day.

Mongolia fact file

Capital: Ulan Bator
Population: 2.6 million

- ▶ Situated between Siberia and China.
- ▶ Terrain varies from desert to mountain. Temperature variations are also extreme.
- ▶ Many Mongolians live a nomadic lifestyle, living in special tents (called gers).
- ▶ Tourism is growing in importance (by approximately 20% in recent years).
- ▶ Most tourists come from China and Russia.

Reading

Cultural differences

1 Work in pairs. Look at this list of 'cultural tips' for tourists when mixing with Mongolian people. Which do you think are 'dos' and which are 'don'ts'?

2 Look at p. 110 and check your answers. Do any of the tips surprise you?

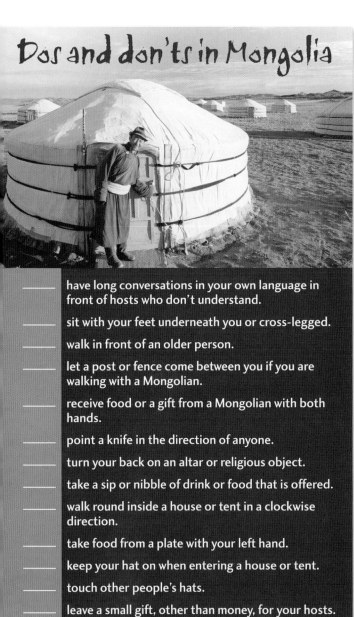

Dos and don'ts in Mongolia

_____ have long conversations in your own language in front of hosts who don't understand.

_____ sit with your feet underneath you or cross-legged.

_____ walk in front of an older person.

_____ let a post or fence come between you if you are walking with a Mongolian.

_____ receive food or a gift from a Mongolian with both hands.

_____ point a knife in the direction of anyone.

_____ turn your back on an altar or religious object.

_____ take a sip or nibble of drink or food that is offered.

_____ walk round inside a house or tent in a clockwise direction.

_____ take food from a plate with your left hand.

_____ keep your hat on when entering a house or tent.

_____ touch other people's hats.

_____ leave a small gift, other than money, for your hosts.

_____ take off your gloves before shaking hands.

3 Complete this table of dos and don'ts for (a) your own country, and (b) another country you know about. Mark dos with a tick (✔), don'ts with a cross (✗), and write – if it doesn't matter.

	(a)	(b)
Smoke in a public building		
Wear a hat in a religious building		
Wear shorts in a religious building		
Point at someone with your finger		
Kiss family or friends in public		
Blow your nose in public		
Eat with your left hand		
Take photos of local people		
Leave food on the plate at the end of the meal		
Arrive on time for an appointment		

Writing

Cultural tips

Write a list of cultural tips for visitors to your country. The list could appear in a guidebook or on a website. Include categories on

- ● eating and drinking
- ● visiting famous and religious buildings
- ● being a guest in someone's house
- ● gestures, body language, and physical contact and space
- ● any other categories you think are important.

Find out

How can you find out about cultural tips for visitors to other countries? Think of a country that you would like to visit. Look at the website of the national tourist office. Does it give any useful advice? Ask your local travel agent for useful cultural advice.

Vocabulary
Escape and enlightenment holidays

1 Choose from these words to label the pictures.

spa	meditation	yoga
shiatsu	massage	aromatherapy
retreat (noun)	t'ai chi	hikes / hiking
anti-aging treatment		

2 Which two words describe a place rather than an activity? Which activities would take place in them?

3 Which of the words would you expect to appear in the brochure descriptions for these holidays?

1 Rio Caliente: Hot springs, Spa and nature resort, Primavera, Mexico

2 Camino de Santiago: The Pilgrimage Route of St James, Spain

3 Dhanakosa Buddhist Retreat, Scotland

4 Work in groups of three. Student A, look at p. 112. Student B, look at p. 116. Student C, look at p. 118.

Tell the others in your group about the holiday and mention

● the location
● what you can do
● any other information.

5 Think of three different people you know and recommend one of the holidays for each of them.

● Language spot
Describing service provision

1 Look at these four ways of describing service provision taken from the texts. In each case find two other examples of the structure.

1 *offers, provides, boasts* (Present Simple)

It **offers** the natural beauty of the forest.

2 *You can* + infinitive

You can enjoy daily yoga and water exercise.

3 Present Simple Passive

The yoga work **is presented** as an important part of meditation practice.

4 Imperative

Depart any day you like from May 1 to October 30.

2 Complete the description using the phrases in the list.

book	provides
is held	you can
offers	

The tour of the Seven Holy Cities of India

_____ ¹ the chance to rediscover your spiritual energy. _____ ² learn about the Hindu religion. _____ ³ visit the sacred town of Haridwar. The spectacular Kumba Mela religious festival _____ ⁴ every twelve years. _____ ⁵ early to avoid disappointment

» Go to **Grammar reference** p.125

Customer care
Ability and suitability

It is important for tourism providers to make sure their customers are able to do the adventure activities they have signed up for. But at the same time, they should allow and encourage people to do things that are 'out of the ordinary'.

1 Do you agree with the statement above?

2 Do you know anyone – e.g. friends or family – who has done an adventure activity or taken a holiday with a difference that you didn't think was suitable?

3 How can tourism providers check their customers' suitability?

4 Are there any situations when a tourism provider should refuse to allow someone to do an activity?

Speaking
Tourist types and holiday types

1 Write four different types of tourist on separate pieces of paper.

EXAMPLE

young single male interested in water sports

2 In groups of three or four, take ten of the types of tourist. Take turns to pick one of them and select a 'holiday with a difference'. Say why you think the tourist would like the holiday. The rest of the group should decide if the match is good.

EXAMPLE

He'll like the windsurfing holiday because he'll be able to develop his skill in water sports.

3 The person with the most accepted matches wins.

Checklist

Assess your progress in this unit. Tick (✓) the statements which are true.

I can understand descriptions of alternative holiday types

I can talk about alternative holiday types

I can ask and talk about past experiences

I can discuss cultural dos and don'ts

I can describe service provision

Key words

Activities
aromatherapy
diving
expedition
hillwalking
massage
meditation
mountain climbing
t'ai chi
whale-watching
white-water rafting
windsurfing
yoga

Places
cattle ranch
health farm
retreat
spa

Other nouns
conservation
enlightenment
mountaineer
volcano
wildlife

Adjective
gastronomic

Next stop

1 How long have we had computers?

2 What are computers used for in the tourism industry?

3 What was the last tourism thing you did on the Internet?

11 Reservations and sales

Take off

1 Can you name the different travel documents on this page?

2 Which of these documents do you need for a holiday abroad?

3 Have you ever lost an important document? Tell your partner – explain which one, where you were, what you did, and what happened in the end.

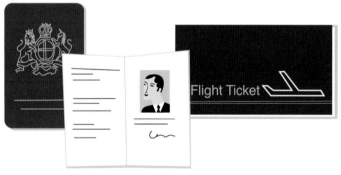

Reading

Holiday bookings – getting the right information

1 Make a list of the information a travel agency sales consultant will need to take when a customer makes a booking for a holiday.

2 Compare your ideas with the list below. Do you have any ideas that are not in the list?

3 The manager uses *etc.* a lot in the memo. What does this mean?

4 Substitute *etc.* with groups of examples from the list.
   a transfers, local excursions, car hire
   b premier class
   c medical condition
   d email address if possible
   e twin, single, family
   f bank transfer, credit card
   g B and B, flight only

Memo	
To: all sales staff	**Subject:** Key reservations data

Please be sure to enter the following key data when taking holiday bookings.

1 date of booking

2 booking reference number

3 full name and contact details of client (postal address, daytime and evening telephone numbers, etc.)

4 number of people in party

5 names of people in party

6 ages of children (2–12 yrs old = discount)

7 dates of outward and return journeys

8 ticket type (e.g. economy, etc.)

9 accommodation – name of hotel / resort

10 number and type of rooms required (double, etc.)

11 special requirements (e.g. children, disabled, etc.)

12 meal basis (full board, half board, etc.)

13 other services (e.g. airport hotel, airport car parking, etc.)

14 method of payment (cash, cheque, etc.)

15 deposit details

Please also get clients to double check all details before signing the booking form.

In this unit
- taking a booking in a travel agency
- computerized reservation systems and the travel agent
- explaining holiday terms and conditions
- 'if' clauses
- handing over tickets to a client

Listening

Taking a booking

1 🎧 Listen to a travel agency sales consultant taking a booking and complete the booking form.

2 Which key data is still missing?

3 What did the travel agent forget to do before Mrs Venables signed the form?

3 When will Mrs Venables get her invoice and what must she do then?

Speaking

Have you decided where to go?

1 Work in pairs. Student A, you are the sales consultant and need to complete the booking form. Student B, you are the client and should think of all of the holiday details the sales consultant will ask. (Hint: Look at the holidays in Unit 10 and choose the one you like most. Now add the details of your family and you are ready to go!)

2 Act out a booking.

3 Change roles and act out a new booking, with Student B as the sales consultant.

Booking reference number
CTS060625797H

Cicerone Travel Services
9 Wilson Court, Bristol

CUSTOMER DETAILS

First name _____ Family name _Venables_

Address _____

Daytime tel no _____ Evening tel no _____

Mobile tel no _____

Email _____

PARTY DETAILS

No of people in party _____ Ages of children _____

Date of outward journey _____ Date of return journey _____

Ticket type _____

ACCOMMODATION

Name of hotel / resort _____

Number of rooms _____

Type of rooms _____

Meal basis _____

Special requirements _____

Other services _____

PAYMENT DETAILS

Method of payment _____

Deposit details _____

Customer's signature _____

Date of booking _____

Writing

Confirming a booking

When a booking is taken by email, it is standard practice to confirm the booking either by email, or by letter.

Use the information from the last activity and send an email to your partner confirming the details of the booking. (If you cannot send an email, send a letter instead.)

accessible (adj) possible to be reached or entered

accounting (adj) connected with the financial arrangements of a company

gateway (n) the place which you must go through in order to get somewhere else

Reading

Computer reservation systems

1 Tourism is full of abbreviations. For example, do you know what CRSs and GDSs are? Do you know the difference between the two?

2 Where can you find out what tourism terms mean?

3 Look at the definition of CRS and GDS. Write T (true) or F (false).

1 Airlines were the first users of CRS.

2 A GDS is a larger version of a CRS.

3 Only airlines and travel agents can have access to GDSs.

4 It is now possible to book a car or a hotel room through a GDS.

5 GDSs give ticket information but cannot produce a valid ticket.

6 GDSs can tell travel agents how many tickets they have sold.

computer reservation system

A computer reservation system, or CRS, is a computerized system used to store and retrieve information and conduct transactions related to travel. Originally designed and operated by airlines, they were later extended to travel agents as a sales channel. Major CRS operations are also known as Global Distribution Systems (GDS). Many systems are now **accessible** to consumers through internet **gateways** for hotel, rental cars, and other services as well as airline tickets.

Today, each system allows an operator to locate and reserve inventory (for instance, an airline seat on a particular route at a particular time), find and process fares / prices applicable to the inventory, generate tickets and travel documents, and generate reports on the transactions for **accounting** or marketing purposes.

Vocabulary

Reservation systems for tourism

Choose the best meaning for each word as it is used in the text on CRS.

1 store = (a) a large shop (b) the place where you keep things until you want to use them (c) to keep something for future use

2 retrieve = (a) to put something back into its original form (b) to get something back (c) to move back to a safe place

3 conduct = (a) to organize and do something (b) to direct the musicians in an orchestra (c) to allow electricity to pass

4 channel =(a) a television station (b) a route that information is sent along (c) the part of a river that boats can pass along

Listening

The origins of CRSs

Clemen works at the *EU de Turismo de Asturias* in Spain. She teaches students there how to use computer-based reservation systems like Amadeus or SABRE.

1 🎧 Listen and complete the table.

System	SABRE	Amadeus	Galileo
Created by			
Created in			
Market share			

2 Clemen mentions a fourth CRS – Worldspan. Listen again and make notes about it.

Hotel bookings

Nowadays, more travel is sold over the Internet than any other consumer product. In America nearly 37 million internet users have already purchased travel products online. Online bookings were expected to reach $63 billion in 2005.

Nothing is free in business – not even a client booking a hotel room. Reservations made directly by the client using the hotel's own website are probably the least expensive. In contrast, a booking made by a travel agent using a GDS is usually the most expensive.

Find out

Which of the big four GDSs do your local travel agencies use most – Amadeus, Sabre, Galileo, Worldspan?

1 Go to a local travel agency and ask them which system they use. Ask them what they like about the system they use, and why they don't use one of the other systems.

2 Report your findings back to your class.

Reading

Abbreviations and codes

1 Look at the computer printout for an air fare between Madrid and Paris.

1 What are the dates for the journey?
2 Can you find the cost of the flight?
3 Is it a return flight? How do you know?
4 What is the opposite of a *return flight*?

2 There are a lot of abbreviations and codes. For example, *RT* means *round-trip* or *return*; *OW* means *one-way*. Find abbreviations that mean

1 adult	7 June
2 advanced	8 minimum stay
3 airline	9 non-refundable
4 check	10 passenger type code
5 euros	11 Sunday
6 flight type code	12 tariff.

Customer care

Putting on the pressure

A

Don't pressure a customer to make a booking if you sense that they are not sure yet. Give them time. Let them go away and think about it. Remember that on average a satisfied customer will tell two friends or members of their family. A dissatisfied customer, in contrast, will tell at least nine people.

B

Customers sometimes need help making up their minds. Put a little pressure on them. Tell them that the booking can only be held for a short time, and you need a decision soon, or they might lose the opportunity altogether. You're the professional, you know what's good for them – so push them a bit.

1 Which of the two statements do you agree with most?

2 What would you actually say to the customer in each situation?

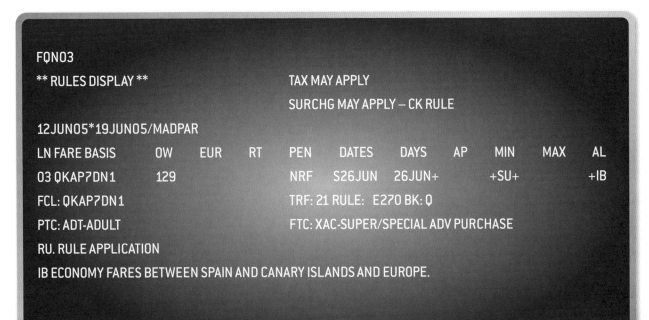

```
FQN03
** RULES DISPLAY **                    TAX MAY APPLY
                                       SURCHG MAY APPLY – CK RULE

12JUN05*19JUN05/MADPAR
LN FARE BASIS      OW     EUR    RT    PEN    DATES    DAYS    AP    MIN    MAX    AL
03 QKAP7DN1       129                  NRF    S26JUN   26JUN+        +SU+          +IB
FCL: QKAP7DN1                          TRF: 21 RULE:  E270 BK: Q
PTC: ADT-ADULT                         FTC: XAC-SUPER/SPECIAL ADV PURCHASE
RU. RULE APPLICATION
IB ECONOMY FARES BETWEEN SPAIN AND CANARY ISLANDS AND EUROPE.
```

avoid (v) to prevent sth happening or to try not to do sth

beforehand (adv) at an earlier time than sth

guarantee (v) to promise that sth will be done or will happen

premium (n) an amount of money that you pay regularly to a company for insurance against accidents, damage, etc.

reserve the right (v) to have or keep a particular power

Reading
The small print

Booking terms and conditions

a We may need to make changes to the information in this brochure as our holidays are planned many months beforehand. If we make any changes before you make your booking, your travel agent will tell you about them before you finish your booking.

b Occasionally we have to change your accommodation. If we make a change after you have made your booking, we will put you into accommodation of the same standard or *higher*, and in a similar type of resort.

c The prices in our brochure were correct at the time of printing, but we **reserve the right** to make changes. If we do this, your travel agent will confirm all price changes before you make your booking.

d If you want to cancel your booking, the person who made the booking must send us written instructions. If you cancel your booking, we may ask you to pay cancellation charges. We will not refund any insurance **premiums** you have paid.

e If you want to change your booking, we will try to help you, but we cannot **guarantee** that we will be able to do this. If you change your booking, we will charge you €15 for each person in your group.

f If you make a booking with us, you must take out suitable insurance, either with us or with another company. If you have a known medical condition, please tell our sales agent when you make your booking.

g We try hard to **avoid** flight delays, but they do sometimes happen. If there is a delay, we will try to provide extra services, food, and accommodation. If we are unable to provide these services for any reason, then we will pay you compensation.

1 Look at the booking conditions. Match these headings with the different conditions.

1 Cancellations
2 Booking changes
3 Compulsory insurance
4 Flight delays
5 If we change your holiday before you leave
6 If we make changes after you have booked your holiday
7 Your holiday price

2 Look at the booking conditions. Which ones are about

1 situations / problems the tour operator may have?
2 situations / problems a tourist may have?
3 situations / problems that happen before a holiday?
4 situations / problems that happen during a holiday?

3 Have you (or your family or friends) ever had a problem when you were on holiday? Tell your partner about it. Where were you? When was it? Who was with you? What happened?

Plastic society
The UK is the biggest card user in Europe, owning 60% of all credit and debit cards. Spain is next with 15%. British adults own an average of 3.5 cards each. There are 246 card transactions every second in Britain, and the average weekly spend is £100.

● Language spot
'If'

1 Look at the booking conditions again.

1 Underline the sentences beginning with *if*.

2 Are these sentences referring to the past, the present, or the future?

3 What verb tense is used in the *if* part of the sentence?

4 What verb forms are used in the other part of the *if* sentences? (Hint: There are *four* different forms.)

2 Match phrases from A with phrases from B to create information and advice for tourists.

A	B
1 If you travel with us to an airport,	a please ask for assistance – we serve more than 1,200 towns and cities in the country.
2 If the destination you want is not listed in this timetable,	b we cannot accept responsibility for your complaint.
3 If you have a problem during the journey,	c tell the driver at the earliest possible moment.
4 If you have a complaint to make during your holiday,	d you may be asked to pay a small surcharge at some hotels on the tour.
5 If you do not contact our representative before the end of your holiday,	e you must allow at least one hour between the coach arrival time and the flight check-in time.
6 If you have asked for a special diet,	f you must contact our representative at the resort before you return home.

3 Complete these four pieces of information / advice for a tourist coming to your country.

1 If you are going to hire a car, …

2 If you come to our country in the high season, …

3 If you are a vegetarian, …

4 If …

>> Go to **Grammar reference** p.126

Pronunciation

1 🎧 Listen to the words and write them in the correct column.

hat /æ/	pay /eɪ/	sit /ɪ/	five /aɪ/
planned	change	in	time

2 Look at all the 'hat' words. Compare them with the 'pay' words. What do you notice about the pronunciation of the letter *a*? When is it like 'hat' and when is it like 'pay'?

3 Look at all the 'sit' words. Compare them with the 'five' words. What do you notice about the pronunciation of the letter *i*? When is it like 'sit' and when is it like 'five'?

Speaking
Explaining booking conditions

Work with a partner. Take turns to be a travel agent sales clerk or a customer. The customer will ask questions about the booking conditions. Here are some questions.

1 Are the prices in the brochure all correct?

2 What happens if we cancel our holiday?

3 Do we need insurance or is that included in the price?

4 Can we change our booking if we have to?

5 Will we definitely get the hotel we asked for in the booking form?

6 What happens if there are flight delays?

The travel agent should look at the booking conditions, but try to answer in her / his own words, like this:

CUSTOMER   *Are the prices in the brochure all correct?*

TRAVEL AGENT   *Well, the prices were right when the brochure was printed, but if they are different now, the tour operator will tell me when I make the booking. And if the prices have changed, I'll tell you before you sign the booking form.*

It's my job

Huayan Ye

Huayan Ye works with Spanish-speaking tourists in China. What does she think of them, and what does she do when she's not with her clients? Read on and find out.

Studies: Spanish, a bit of tourism, and international relations at Beijing University.

Job: Working in the biggest tourism company in China – it's called CTS – in the inbound tourism department. I look after Spanish tourists and tourists from Latin America. We offer them tourism services – hotel reservations, transfers, visits in China ...

Why tourism? I like talking to people. I want to show foreign visitors the best of China.

Likes: I really like marketing and sales. Our department doesn't just look after the Spanish. It also studies the Chinese market. Right now it's growing a lot. China is one of the safest destinations in the world, and the Chinese are kind and friendly.

Clients: Our Latin-American clients are very friendly. Our Spanish clients are a little bit more demanding! The Spanish have a lot more experience travelling, and they know so much about tourism. That's why they are demanding, but that's good for us.

Free time: Young people in China like to go out for a drink, go shopping, go to stores, study English. I like reading, listening to music, and I study Latin-American dance – salsa, tango. And like all young women, we like to buy clothes, shoes, cosmetics ...

Listening

Handing over tickets

PASSENGER			ISSUING AGENT				
BORDONI, GIORGIO MR			CANTRAVEL TORONTO CA 8541				

PORT	CARRIER	FLIGHT #	DATE	DEP	ARR	STATUS	FARE CL
TORONTO YYZ	AIRCAN	AC094	12AUG	2335	1210	OK	RAS
BUENOS AIRES EZE	AIRCAN	AC093	23AUG	1655	0635	OK	WAI
-- VOID --							
-- VOID --							

RESTRICTIONS	BOOKING REF
NONE	KMH155.5 HA OERN56.9ERF SADM CDA

CURRENCY	FARE	TAX	TOTAL
CAN$	3851	99.74	3950.74

1 Look at the flight ticket and find

1 the name of the passenger
2 the date of outbound travel
3 the outbound flight number
4 the origin of the outbound flight
5 the destination of the outbound flight
6 the flight times
7 the cost of the ticket.

2 🎧 Listen to the travel agent handing over the ticket. Which of these pieces of information does he confirm with the client?

3 What does Mr Bordoni ask the travel agent about?

4 🎧 Listen again and complete the dialogue.

T Here's your ticket. Let's just go through the
_____¹. So, that's Toronto–Buenos Aires
_____², leaving August 12 on _____³
AC094. _____⁴ Toronto at 23.35h and
_____⁵ Buenos Aires the next day at 12.10.

B That's not too bad.

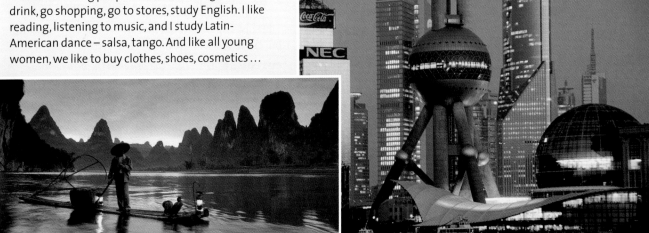

T No, it's a good flight. Then there's your return. That's August 23, flight AC093. _____⁶ Buenos Aires at 16.55. _____⁷ Toronto 06.35. One passenger – yourself. Total _____⁸ $3,950.74.

B Ouch! That *includes* taxes, no?

T That includes taxes, _____⁹, and _____¹⁰.

B And it *is* _____¹¹?

T One *hundred* per cent refundable, Mr Bordoni. If you don't go, you don't _____¹². And as I said, you can change the dates of travel _____¹³ _____¹⁴ two hours before take off.

B OK. That's good. Will you _____¹⁵ the company directly?

T No problem.

B Then … then that's everything, I think.

T Good.

B Thanks for your help.

T Our pleasure, Mr Bordoni.

Speaking
Checking the details

1 Think about a return flight you would like to take. Complete the blank ticket with details of your journey. Make sure all of the information is properly covered.

2 Give your ticket to your partner.

3 When your partner is ready, ask for your ticket. Your partner should check all the details with you. Correct any details that are wrong.

4 Change roles and take the role of the travel agent.

Checklist

Assess your progress in this unit. Tick (✓) the statements which are true.

- I can take a holiday booking from a client in a travel agency
- I understand basic ideas that I read or hear about GDSs
- I can ask for the meaning of travel abbreviations and codes
- I can explain holiday terms and conditions
- I can issue a ticket and check the booking details with the client

Key words

Nouns

abbreviation
balance
cancellation
CRS – computerized reservation system
deposit details
fare
GDS – global distribution system

insurance
inventory
key data
maximum stay
meal basis
minimum stay
surcharge
tariff
tax

Verbs

cancel
confirm
guarantee
issue (a ticket)
retrieve (data)
store (data)

Next stop

1 Do you like being in airports or stations or do you get nervous before you travel?

2 What do you do while you're waiting in airports or stations? What facilities do you normally use?

3 Have you ever had a problem at the start of a journey? How did you solve it?

12 Airport departures

Take off

1 How many airports have you been to?

2 What's your favorite airport? Why?

3 Where do you think would be the most interesting place to work in an airport? Where would be the most dangerous?

Where in the world?

1 Does the plan show the departures level or the arrivals level?

2 What happens when travellers depart from and arrive at an airport? Divide the following into departure and arrival procedures and put them in the order in which they occur.

a passport control
b board the plane
c security check
d immigration
e departure lounge
f arrivals hall
g baggage reclaim
h check-in desk
i departure gate
j get off the plane (disembark)
k customs

3 Is the airport similar to your local airport?

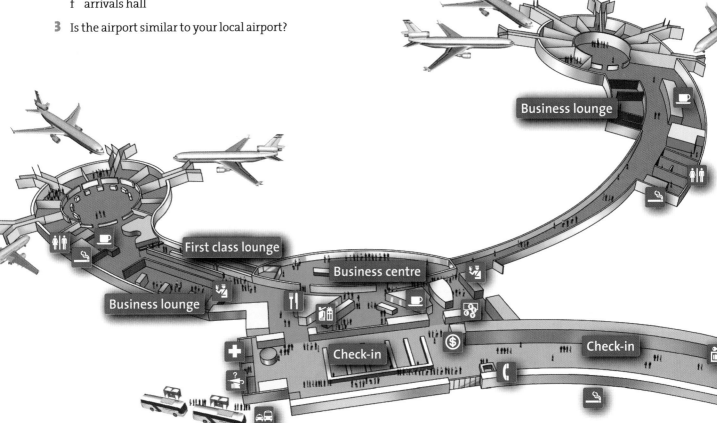

Business lounge

First class lounge

Business centre

Business lounge

Check-in

Check-in

In this unit
- airport facilities, services, and procedures
- responding politely to questions and requests
- airport dialogues
- giving orders, stopping people doing something

Vocabulary

Airport facilities and services

1 What do the symbols of airport facilities represent?

2 Which symbol represents a place where

a you can store your baggage?
b you can get emergency medical treatment?
c you can rent a car?
d you may have your luggage searched?
e you might find something you have lost?

3 Match the words in the list with the symbols.

a hotel reservations	j lost property	r lifts
b immigration	k smoking area	s bar
c luggage trolleys	l post office	t first aid
d restaurant / cafe	m information	u customs
e bureau de change	n hairdressers	v toilets
f baggage store	o escalators	w telephones
g email and Internet	p departures	x arrivals
h railway station	q shops	y car rental
i cashier		

4 Work in pairs. Five services or facilities do not have a symbol. Design suitable symbols, and compare with the class.

Reading

Working in airports

1 Make a list of the different jobs there are in an airport. Which job would you most / least like to do?

2 Read the article for people training in tourism and complete the missing sections with the extracts below.

Inside tourism: Getting an airport job

When people think about working in the air travel industry they usually think of flight attendants and pilots – the cabin crew and the flight crew. But there are many other job opportunities at airports. These can include working in the various _____ ¹, or more specifically tourism related services, such as the _____ ².

The work of the airline ground crew includes _____ ³ until they board the plane and are handed over to the cabin crew. Most employers will expect ground crew to have a good basic education, including a good level of English. You should have a pleasant helpful personality. Previous experience in a job which involves working with the public (such as _____ ⁴) is preferred.

As with travel consultants and cabin crew, ground crew are usually employed on permanent contracts but often work shifts. Free and discounted flights are usually offered after a probationary period.

Some jobs at the airport do not involve contact with the public. Examples of these are _____ ⁵.

For more information on getting a job at an airport, you should …

a information desk, the bureau de change, the check-in desk, the security check, and customs and immigration

b shops, hotels, restaurants, and banks

c baggage handlers, mechanics, and drivers

d restaurants, bars, and shops

e selling tickets, checking in passengers, dealing with enquiries, and supervising passengers

Listening

An airport worker

Ali Ghoshal was born and brought up in Pakistan. He now works at London's Heathrow airport as an aircraft technician as part of the *turn-around team*.

1 🎧 Listen to the interview and answer the questions.

1 What does the *turn-around team* do?
2 How many people are in the team?
3 Does Ali have any special qualifications?
4 What is the main stress in his job?
5 What does he like most?
6 What does he like least?
7 Does he get any special 'perks' or benefits?
8 What does he plan to do in the future?

2 🎧 Listen again and complete the questions that the interviewer asks.

1 What does _____ ?
2 How many _____ ?
3 What qualifications _____ ?
4 Is it _____ ?
5 What do you _____ ?
6 And _____ ?
7 So you're _____ ?
8 Do you _____ ?

Find out

Find out about your nearest airport and complete the fact file.

Vocabulary

Airport language

1 Which airport workers are shown in the pictures?

2 Complete the questions with the words in the list, and say where each question would be asked.

sharp objects	ticket	help	board
meeting point	window	aisle	suitcase
purpose	baggage	passport	help
checking in	landed	meeting	

1 Can I have your _____ and _____ ?
2 Has the flight _____ yet?
3 Did you pack your _____ yourself?
4 Are you _____ someone?
5 What is the _____ of your visit?
6 Are you carrying any _____ in your hand luggage?
7 Could you _____ me?
8 Can I _____ you?
9 Has your _____ been in your possession at all times?
10 Are there any _____ seats available?
11 Can you tell me where the _____ is?
12 Is it too late to _____ the plane?
13 Are you _____ any bags today?
14 Would you like an _____ seat?

3 Which questions are asked by passengers?

FACT FILE

Name of airport: ....
Airport code: ....
Airlines operating: ....
Information – telephone number:
....
Information – website / email:
....
Lost luggage – telephone number: ....
Distance from main city / cities in region: ....

Transport options to city:
....
Cost of return trip to city:
....
Hotel options (at or near airport):
....
Restaurant facilities: ....
Shopping facilities: ....
Business services: ....
VIP lounge: ....
Car hire companies operating:
Car park fees (short stay / long stay): ....

The world's busiest airports

The world's busiest airports in 2002 (millions of passengers)				
1	Atlanta (ATL)	75.8	5 Tokyo (HND)	58.7
			6 Dallas / Fort Worth (DFW)	55.2
2	Chicago (ORD)	66.8	7 Frankfurt (FRA)	48.6
3	Los Angeles (LAX)	61.0	8 Paris (CDG)	48.0
4	London (LHR)	60.7	9 Amsterdam (AMS)	39.5
			10 Denver (DEN)	36.1

● Language spot

Responding politely to questions and requests

1 Match the following responses by airport workers with the five passenger questions in *Vocabulary* **2**.

  a Certainly. How can I help?

  b I'm afraid it is. The cabin doors have been locked.

  c No, I'm sorry, it hasn't. There's been a delay.

  d Yes, of course. It's just over there, next to the newsagents.

  e I'm afraid there aren't. The flight's very full.

2 Which expressions are used as more polite alternatives to *yes* and *no*?

3 Practise the five exchanges in pairs.

4 Note how the airport worker gives a reason when saying *no*. This makes the negative more polite.

Think of a reason for saying *no* to the following questions.

  1 Can we smoke here?

  2 Can I go to the front of the queue?

  3 Is it OK to take my guitar on as hand luggage?

  4 Is there any chance of an upgrade to First Class?

5 In pairs, practise the four situations above.

6 Write down three or four questions that a passenger might ask – include at least one where you would expect a negative response. Ask your questions to a partner and act out the dialogue.

» Go to **Grammar reference** p.126

Listening

Two airport dialogues

1 Listen to these two airport dialogues.

  1 Where do they take place?

  2 Note down the flight numbers, gate numbers, and cities that are mentioned.

2 Listen again and complete the dialogues.

CONVERSATION A

A Could you _____¹? I'm trying to find out if a flight has arrived or not.

B _____². Are you meeting someone?

A Yes, my brother. He was due in on _____³ from _____⁴. Has it arrived yet?

B Yes, _____⁵. Let me check the _____⁶. Here it is. It arrived an hour ago. He should be coming through _____⁷ about now.

A Right, I'll go there. _____⁸, you say?

B Yes, or if he's not at _____⁹, try the _____¹⁰.

A That's a good idea. Can _____¹¹ where the meeting point is?

B _____¹². It's just over there, next to the newsagent's.

A Thanks for your help.

B _____¹³.

CONVERSATION B

C Hello. Can I have your passport and _____¹?

D Here you are.

C Thank you. Are you _____² any bags today?

D Just this one. The other's _____³.

C Can you put it on the _____⁴? Thanks. Did you _____⁵ yourself?

D Yes, I did.

C Has anyone _____⁶ your luggage in any way?

D No, they haven't.

C Are you carrying any _____⁷ such as nail scissors?

D No, I'm not. Can _____⁸ if there are any window seats available?

C No, _____⁹ there aren't. The flight's very full. Would you like an aisle seat?

D Yes, that'll do.

C OK. Here's your _____¹⁰. You'll be boarding through _____¹¹ in 30 minutes. Have a _____¹².

D Thank you.

Speaking

The check-in and information desks

Work in pairs. Student A, look at p.113. Student B, look at p.114.

compensation (n) money that you pay to sb because you have injured him/her or lost or damaged his/her property

refund (n) a sum of money that is paid back to you, especially because you have paid too much or you are not happy with sth you have bought

volunteer (n) a person who offers or agrees to do sth without being forced or paid to do it

Reading

Air passenger rights

1 What things can go wrong for air passengers? Think about: before boarding, during the flight, after landing.

2 Now look at the front page of a European Commission leaflet about air passengers' rights. What do you think air passengers have a right to in each of the four categories?

If you are denied boarding, the airline must…

If your flight is cancelled, the airline must…

Having problems with your journey?

The European Union (EU) has strengthened your rights. Here are the most important.

IF THINGS GO WRONG …
The EU has created a set of rights to ensure air passengers are treated fairly.
The airline operating your flight is responsible for transporting you and your baggage, and must respect your rights.

DENIED BOARDING
Were you denied boarding because the airline did not have enough seats on the flight?

CANCELLED FLIGHT
Has your flight been cancelled?

LONG DELAYS
Is your flight delayed for two hours or more?

BAGGAGE
Has your checked-in baggage been damaged, delayed, or lost?

DENIED BOARDING AND CANCELLATION
If you are denied boarding or your flight is cancelled, the airline operating your flight must offer you financial **compensation** and assistance. These rights apply, provided you check in on time, for any flight, including charter:

- from an EU airport, or
- to an EU airport from one outside the EU, when operated by an EU airline

DENIED BOARDING
When there are too many passengers for the seats available, an airline must first ask for **volunteers** to give up their seats in return for agreed benefits. These must include the choice of either **refund** of your ticket or alternative transport to your destination.

If you are not a volunteer, the airline must pay you compensation of:

- €250 for flights of 1,500 km or less
- €400 for longer flights within the EU, and for other flights between 1,500 km and 3,500 km
- €600 for flights over 3,500 km outside the EU.

The airline must also give you:

- a choice of either a refund of your ticket (with a free flight back to your initial point of departure when relevant) or
- alternative transport to your destination, and meals and refreshments, hotel accommodation when necessary (including transfers), and communication facilities.

CANCELLATION
Whenever your flight is cancelled, the operating airline must give you:

- a choice of either a refund or your ticket (with a free flight back to your initial point of departure when relevant) or
- alternative transport to your destination, and meals and refreshments, hotel accommodation when necessary (including transfers), and communication facilities.

The airline may also have to compensate you at the same level as for denied boarding, unless it gives you sufficient advance notice. You shall be informed about alternative transport.

3 Work in two groups. Group A, read about 'Denied boarding' and 'Cancellation'. Group B, read about 'Long delays' and 'Baggage'.

1 Check to see if your answers in **2** were correct.

2 Find out the level of compensation that the airline must provide.

4 Explain what you have discovered to a student from the other group.

Refunds may be in cash, by bank transfer or cheque or, with your signed agreement, in travel vouchers, and must be paid within seven days.

If you do not receive these rights, complain immediately to the airline operating the flight.

LONG DELAYS / IMMEDIATE ASSISTANCE
If you check in on time for any flight, including charters: from an EU airport, or to an EU airport from one outside the EU, when operated by an EU airline and if the airline operating the flight expects a delay

- of two hours or more, for flights of 1,500 km or less
- of three hours or more, for longer flights between 1,500 and 3,500 km
- of four hours or more for flights over 3,500 km

the airline must give you meals and refreshments, hotel accommodation when necessary (including transfers), and communication facilities.

When the delay is five hours or more, the airline must also offer to refund your ticket (with a free flight back to your initial point of departure when relevant).

If you do not receive these rights, complain immediately to the airline operating the flight.

BAGGAGE
You may claim up to €1,000 for damage caused by the destruction, damage, loss, or delay of your baggage on a flight by an EU airline, anywhere in the world. If the airline does not agree with your claim, you may go to court.

For damage to checked-in baggage, you must claim in writing within seven days of its return and for delayed baggage within 21 days of its return.

Speaking
Incident and action log

1 In groups, look at this airline 'incident and action log'. For each of the incidents, decide if the airline acted correctly according to the European Commission leaflet.

2 Have any incidents like this ever happened to you, or someone you know? Tell the rest of the group about it.

Incident	Passenger action	Airline action
1 Five passengers overbooked on flight from London to Paris	No passengers volunteered to go on to alternative flight	Passengers selected randomly and put on alternative flight (three hours later). Free meal and drink given as compensation, plus €50 voucher for the Gift Shop.
2 Flight from Rome to New York cancelled at last minute due to technical problems	All passengers moved on to flight on next day	Hotel accommodation given (plus meals and transfers). In addition compensation of €250 paid to each passenger.
3 Flight from Zurich to Dublin delayed by one hour and 30 minutes	n/a	Free drink given to all passengers.
4 Flight from Madrid to Tokyo delayed by seven hours	Nearly all passengers agreed to wait, but two wanted to cancel and get a refund	Meals and refreshments given, plus offer of airport hotel accommodation. No refunds given.
5 Baggage lost on Bonn to London flight	Passenger claimed €2,000 compensation	Passenger given €1,000 compensation and a 10% discount voucher for a future flight.
6 Suitcase damaged, and some contents broken and missing (on same flight as 5)	Passenger made verbal report to clerk, but written claim received eight days later	Passenger given €100 compensation.

Customer care

Care or control?

1 At airports customers must be cared for, but they must also be controlled. Can you think of examples of where *care* and *control* are needed in an airport?

2 What are the safety or security risks in the cartoon?

3 What should the member of staff say to the passenger?

Listening

Two more airport dialogues

1 Work in pairs. What problems can passengers have at airports (a) with their luggage, (b) if they arrive late?

2 🎧 Listen to two dialogues.

1 In which dialogue is the airport employee showing care and in which is she showing control?

2 Make notes on the problems.

3 What solution(s) is / are offered in each case?

3 🎧 Listen again. Complete the sentences. You may need more than one word per space.

1 _____ to the oversized baggage desk – sometimes bags go there _____ .

2 Yes, I _____ .

3 In the meantime, _____ fill in this form, so we can trace it?

4 If you _____ wait over there, _____ this out.

5 Excuse me, sir. I'm _____ , but you _____ through there.

6 I'm afraid _____ – the cabin doors have been shut.

7 Sir, _____ the barrier! If you do, _____ call security.

8 Now, _____ my colleague at the airline desk over there, _____ that you get on the next available flight.

● Language spot

Giving orders and stopping people doing something

1 Look at the different language areas used in the table below.

Language area	(Giving an order/ instruction)	(Stopping someone doing something)
1 Imperative	Take off your jacket!	Don't smoke here!
2 *Can you / could you?*	Can you take off your jacket?	Can you please not smoke here?
3 *I'm sorry / I'm afraid*	I'm sorry, but you'll have to take off your jacket.	I'm sorry, but you can't smoke here. *or* I'm afraid this is a no smoking area.
4 *If* clause	If you take off your jacket, we can let you through. *or* If you could just take off your jacket.	If you want to smoke, you'll have to go to the special area.

2 Which of the examples seem firm but polite, and which seem firm but direct?

3 Find other examples in the listening script on p.136.

4 Write similar sentences for these situations.

> Go to departure gate immediately

> Wait behind the yellow line

➤➤ Go to **Grammar reference** p.126

Pronunciation

When we deal with the public we usually want to sound firm but polite.

1 🎧 Listen and decide whether these sentences are (a) firm but polite *or* (b) firm but too direct.

	(a)	(b)
1 Can you take off your jacket?	☐	☐
2 Can you take off your jacket?	☐	☐
3 I'm sorry, but you can't smoke here.	☐	☐
4 I'm sorry, but you can't smoke here.	☐	☐
5 If you could just take off your jacket.	☐	☐
6 If you could just take off your jacket.	☐	☐
7 I'm afraid this is a no-smoking area.	☐	☐
8 I'm afraid this is a no-smoking area.	☐	☐

2 🎧 Listen and repeat. Be firm but polite.

3 Try saying the following in a firm but polite voice.
1 Can you put your bag in the tray?
2 If you could take your watch off.
3 I'm sorry, but you can't take photos here.
4 I'm afraid you can't use your mobile here.

Speaking

Controlling passengers

1 Look at the situations. For each one, decide why it is wrong, give a possible reason for the passengers behaviour, and say what level of firmness is required.
1 Passenger not waiting behind line at immigration
2 Passenger not wanting to take off shoes at security check
3 Passenger refusing to open suitcase at customs
4 Passenger going through a door marked 'Private'
5 *Think of another*

2 In pairs, role-play the situations. Passengers should be insistent; employees should be firm but polite.

Checklist

Assess your progress in this unit. Tick (✓) the statements which are true.

☐ I can describe airport facilities and services

☐ I can respond politely to questions and requests

☐ I can understand and participate in a variety of airport dialogues

☐ I can give orders and stop people doing something

Key words

Airport staff
baggage handler
cabin crew
ground crew
mechanic

Airport places and procedures

aisle	departure lounge
baggage reclaim	escalator
barrier	immigration
bureau de change	lost property
customs	passport control
departure gate	security check

Other nouns

boarding pass	seatbelt
passenger flow	trolley
scales	

Verb
land

Next stop

1 What encounters have you had as a tourist or visitor in any of these places: a travel agency, a tourist information office, an airport, a hotel, or when using a website?

2 Who did you meet?

3 How did they help you? How do you rate the service they provided?

Pairwork activities

Unit 1 p.8

Job skills

Student A

Information	Jamyang Shiwah	Maria Sanchez
Nationality	Tibetan	
Age	29	
Job	Mountain tour guide	
Qualities and skills	Physically fit Knows the mountains	
Working hours	Varies. 24 hours a day when on an expedition	
Typical daily tasks	Meets and greets the travellers; guides them along the route; looks after them; interprets	
Things he / she enjoys about the job	The mountains, the outdoor life, meeting different people	
Relaxing after work	Plays music	
Own holidays	With his family in the city	

Unit 2 p.14

The biggest spenders and the biggest earners

Student A

Top 10 Tourism Spenders

Position	Country	Expenditure ($ billion)
1	the USA	62.1
2	Germany	48.1
3	the United Kingdom	36.4
4	Japan	35.6
5	Spain	24.7
6	France	18.4
7	Italy	17.7
8	Austria	13.5
9	Canada	12.7
10	the Netherlands	11.3

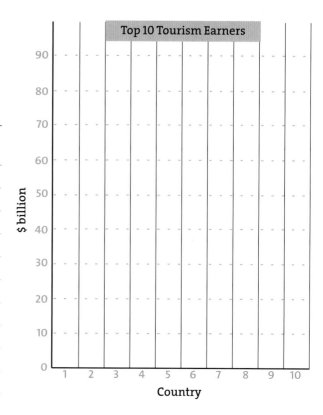

Unit 2 p.19

Describing a destination

SOUTH AFRICA

Location and geographic features
- southern hemisphere
- between Atlantic and Indian Oceans
- 1¼ million square kilometres
- central plateau (or 'veld') with mountains to the south and east
- dramatic coastline and many beaches

Climate
- warm, temperate, and dry
- 65% of the country has less than 50 cm rainfall a year

Tourist attractions
- mountains and fabulous beaches
- vineyards
- wildlife reserves (e.g. Kruger National Park – 137 mammal species, 430 bird species)
- Cape Town – lively city life and culture

Other
- tourism is a major industry
- problem of rising crime in some parts

SEYCHELLES

Location and geographic features
- middle of Indian Ocean
- 1,500 km east of Africa
- 115 islands
- capital is Victoria on island of Mahe

Climate
- tropical oceanic
- only small change in temperature throughout year
- rainfall is low, especially in June, July, and August

Tourist attractions
- fabulous beaches (e.g. at Praslin)
- the climate
- unique flora and fauna, including the giant tortoise
- honeymoon island ('paradise')

Other
- economy relies on tourism
- tourism employs 30% of the workforce

Unit 3 p.23

Talking to tour operators

Student A

1 You are the tour operator. Use the information in the box to answer your partner's questions.

Tour feature	Tour: Beaches of Kerala (Southern India)
Tour area + type	Beach resort holiday
Air fares	Not included. Client must organize
Transfers	Transfers to and from airport on first and last day included. Private minibus used
Meals	Breakfast & evening meal. Breakfast & lunch on day of departure
Hotels	All hotels locally owned and managed. Maximum size = 24 rooms. All hotels have private gardens and luxury-class services, etc.
Groups (= 7+ people)	Not accepted. Maximum 4 people per booking. No minimum
Discount for groups	None
Travel agent's commission	10%
Brochures	Available next month for next season

2 Now change roles. You are the travel agent. Ask your partner about culture and folklore tours to Mexico. Use the ideas in the 'Tour feature' column of the box to guide you.

Unit 5 p.42

Suggesting alternatives and making a recommendation

Student A

1 You are a sales consultant. Your partner is a customer. Suggest alternatives from the box for the situation the customer describes. Finish by recommending the best option.

	Suggestions
Situation 1	A trip to the Pyramids and the Nile A pass to the Formula 1 race at Monaco A beginner's course in scuba diving [Your own suggestion]
Situation 2	A round-the-world flight A safari and beach package in Kenya A cruise around the Caribbean [Your own suggestion]
Situation 3	An opera tour of Germany and Italy A tour of the Greek Islands A trip to Patagonia [Your own suggestion]

2 Now you are the customer. Go into the travel agency and ask for advice for each situation. Ask the sales consultant for at least three alternatives for each situation.

Situation 4 You want a very special holiday for your parents who are about to celebrate their 25th wedding anniversary.

Situation 5 You and your friends have just left university. You want to travel together around Canada.

Situation 6 You want a family holiday for you and your wife / husband and your two small children.

Unit 5 p.39

Investigating a client's needs

Sales consultant

You are the travel agent. There are two customers browsing in your agency. Go up to them and begin to establish rapport. Invite them to have a seat and then use open questions to investigate their initial needs. Make notes of what they want.

Unit 4 p.35

Changes in tourist motivation

Student A

Survey A: What were the main reasons for your holiday journey? (1986)

1 Switching off, relaxation
2 Getting away from everyday life, and having a change of scene
3 Recovering strength
4 Experiencing nature
5 Having time for one another (friends or family)
6 Getting sunshine, escaping from bad weather
7 Being with other people, having company
8 Eating well
9 Having fun and entertainment
10 Doing what I want, being free

Unit 10 p.89

Cultural differences

Don't	have long conversations in your own language in front of hosts who don't understand.
Do	sit with your feet underneath you or cross-legged.
Don't	walk in front of an older person.
Don't	let a post or fence come between you if you are walking with a Mongolian.
Do	receive food or a gift from a Mongolian with both hands.
Don't	point a knife in the direction of anyone.
Don't	turn your back on an altar or religious object.
Do	take a sip or nibble of drink or food that is offered.
Do	walk round inside a house or tent in a clockwise direction.
Don't	take food from a plate with your left hand.
Do	keep your hat on when entering a house or tent.
Don't	touch other people's hats.
Do	leave a small gift, other than money, for your hosts.
Do	take off your gloves before shaking hands.

Unit 7 p.62

Giving information about hotels

Student A

Home Hotels Resorts FAQ

H10 Las Palmeras (Tenerife) ★★★★

The H10 Las Palmeras hotel is located in Playa de las Americas, surrounded by generous subtropical gardens with direct access to the seaside-promenade and only 15 km from the airport.

Food & drink

In the hotel you can find the 'Las Palmeras' Restaurant, where there is a buffet with show cooking, a Barbecue Restaurant near the swimming pool, a Pool Bar, the 'Big Ben' Bar, which offers evening entertainment, a Piano Bar in the Hall, and the 'Ballena' Bar , a snack-bar near the beach.

Sports & leisure

The hotel has two swimming pools (one heated in winter), with a special section for children, three tennis courts, ping pong, and billiards.

Facilities & services

Hairdresser, Internet corner, private parking, souvenir shops, car rental, money exchange, room service, TV, games room, meeting rooms, and day and night-time entertainment are also available in the hotel.

Unit 7 p.67

Taking a telephone booking

Caller 1
guest name: Wei-Wei Lai
room type: single, smoking
contact telephone: 669 374 370 7713
arrival: Thursday 23
departure: Monday 27
credit card type: Visa
card holder's name: Wei-Wei Lai
card number: 6381 8352 7497 6832
expiry date: 07/08

Caller 2
guest name: Regina Loreto
room type: double, non-smoking (at the back of the hotel)
contact telephone: 0034 93 863 5569
arrival: Monday 13
departure: Friday 17
credit card type: American Express
card holder's name: Regina Loreto
card number: 7400 6583 4545 4890
expiry date: 01/09

Unit 8 p.71

Do you SWOT?

Student A

transport and access – transport links with the rest of the country are very good (S)
accommodation – already good and getting better (S)
restaurants, etc. – good and varied but not geared to tourism yet (O)
local food – original and tasty but not well-known (O)
nightlife and clubbing – not very good and not very safe (W)
museums and art galleries – very good in the other city in the area (T)
activities for families – a very good range of activities (S)
the weather – unpredictable summers, cold winters. (T)
marketing potential – very high but not yet used to its full potential (O)
marketing strategy – no marketing strategy (W)
current advertising – only brochures and a poor web page (W)
the image of the city – poor, and often identified with industry and contamination (W)

Unit 9 p.79

The air travel route map

Team A

Baggage: Personal possessions taken on to a plane by a passenger, including checked and hand luggage

Connecting flight: A segment of a flight that requires a passenger to change planes, but not change carriers

Direct flight: A flight that does not involve a change of flight number

Fly-Drive package: A package that includes the cost of both the flight and hire of a car at the destination

Hub: A central airport used as a connecting point to direct passengers to their other destinations. Madrid is the hub for the Spanish airline *Iberia*

Non-stop flight: A flight without any stops

Open-jaw trip: A return air ticket that allows you to fly into a country at one airport, and leave the country by a different airport

Return trip: An air journey that departs from and arrives back at the same airport

Stopover: An interruption to a trip lasting twelve or more hours

Terminal: The airport building that has all the facilities for passengers that are arriving or departing

Unit 10 p.88

Questions on Antarctica

Student A

Ask B these questions. Make notes and ask for clarification and more details if necessary.

1 Where do ships leave from?
2 Do we get a chance to go ashore?

Answer B's questions using this information. Give as much detail as possible.

ANTARCTICA

No documentation or visas are required to visit Antarctica, but if your cruise stops off at other countries en route, visas and documentation may be required for them.

A variety of passenger ships sail to Antarctica and the choice of ship can make a big difference to your journey and experiences.

Antarctic cruises aren't like other more well-known cruises to warmer climates with discos and showbiz entertainment, though the larger the ship, the more likely there is to be entertainment provided.

What you will find is a number of very well informed and experienced cruise guides working on the ship who will give lectures on a regular basis about various aspects of Antarctic history and natural history. These will also often be around to socialize in the evenings along with some of the ship's crew and captain.

Unit 10 p.90

Escape and enlightenment holidays

Student A

RIO CALIENTE — **Hot Springs – Spa and Nature Resort Primavera, Mexico**

Home
Therapies
Activities
Map
Booking

Rio Caliente is a natural hot springs spa and retreat centre, only 45 minutes from the international airport of Guadalajara, Mexico. Situated on the slopes of an ancient valley, it offers the natural beauty of the forest and mountains and boasts a perfect mountain climate. Rio Caliente provides the ideal secluded location for the spa-goer seeking rest, relaxation, and rejuvenation.

At Rio Caliente, you can enjoy daily yoga and water exercise, guided nature hikes, soaks in hot mineral water, horseback excursions, massage, aromatherapy, beauty and anti-aging treatments.

Recharge your spirit and your imagination. Recharge your body and soul. Come to Rio Caliente!

Unit 12 p.103

The check-in and information desks

Student A

1 You are a check-in clerk. Look at the departures board and seat availability notes and answer Student B's questions.

Flight	To	Sched.	Actual	Gate	Seats available
UA900	Frankfurt	08.25	08.25	G7	All
KL605	Amsterdam	10.00	10.00	A8	No window, no front
DL8599	Paris	10.15	10.25	A7	No window, some aisle but not two together. Front only
UA926	Paris	11.30	11.50	G9	Aisle. Window (over wing only)
BA284	London	11.40	13.10	?	All

REMINDERS:
* Check passenger has correct flight
* Check in luggage (hand luggage = one bag only)
* Ask security questions
* Give boarding pass and gate number
* Point out if flight is on time

2 Now change roles. You are a customer meeting a traveller. Ask the information clerk questions to find out about the following.

Customer meeting traveller 1
Meeting: Ms Amanda French (business contact)
Flight: from Auckland (NZ008?)
Note: VIP travelling first class

Customer meeting traveller 2
Meeting: Doris Marshall (your grandmother)
Flight: UA955
Note: never flown before

Customer meeting traveller 3
Meeting: Ko Miyuki and family
Flight: from London but not sure of number
Note: worried because you arrived late

Customer meeting traveller 4
Meeting: Thorsten Krebs from Germany
Flight: VS019 from London
Note: needs to be at very important meeting at 16.30

Unit 2 p.14

The biggest spenders and the biggest earners

Student B

Top 10 Tourism Earners

Position	Country	Receipts ($ billion)
1	the USA	85.2
2	Spain	36.4
3	France	33.4
4	Italy	27.5
5	the United Kingdom	23.1
6	Austria	18.0
7	Germany	16.3
8	China	16.2
9	Greece	13.1
10	Canada	10.8

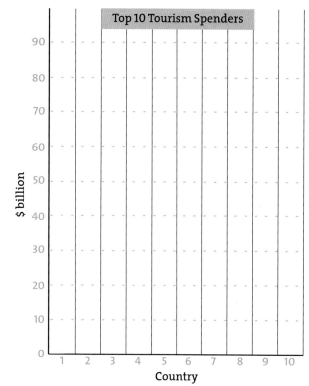

Unit 12 p.103

The check-in and information desks

Student B

1 You are a passenger. Ask the check-in clerk about departures and seat availability.

Passenger 1
Flight: UA900 to Frankfurt
Preferred seat: window
Luggage: two bags as hand luggage

Passenger 2
Flight: KL605 to Amsterdam
Preferred seat: window
Luggage: very large suitcase

Passenger 3
Flight: DL8599 to Paris
Preferred seat: no preference, but two together
Luggage: one to check and one hand luggage each

Passenger 4
Flight: BA284
Preferred seat: no preference
Luggage: hand luggage only (in a hurry to get to appointment in London)

2 Now change roles. You are the information clerk. Look at the arrivals board and answer Student A's questions.

Flight	From	Sched.	Actual	Gate	Remarks
NZ008	Auckland	12.20	13.45	G	In customs
UA955	London	12.35	12.50	G	In customs / cleared
CX872	Hong Kong	13.35	13.20	A	In customs
UA324	New York	13.50	14.20	A	Landed
VS019	London	14.00	15.30	G	Delayed

Time now is 14.30.

Unit 3 p.23

Talking to tour operators

Student B

1 You are a travel agent. Ask the tour operator questions about package holidays to the beaches of Kerala in Southern India. Use the ideas in the 'Tour feature' column of the box below to guide you.

2 Now change roles. You are the tour operator. Use the information in the box to answer your partner's questions.

Tour feature	Tour: Mexico and its folklore guided tour
Tour area + type	Culture and folklore circular tour from Mexico City
Air fares	Tourist-class ticket included
Transfers	Transfers to and from airport and all transfers during tour included. Coaches and local taxis used
Meals	All meals included except on the two free days when only breakfast included
Hotels	Only luxury-class international hotels used
Groups (= 12+ people)	Accepted
Discount for groups	7.5% for group 12–20 pax. 9% for groups 20+ pax
Travel agent's commission	9%
Brochures	Will send within 48 hours of receiving address

Unit 5 p.42

Suggesting alternatives and making a recommendation

Student B

1 You are a customer. Go into the travel agency and ask for advice for each situation. Ask the sales consultant for at least three alternatives for each situation.

Situation 1 You are looking for an incentive trip for your company's best worker.

Situation 2 You are about to get married and are looking for a place to go on your honeymoon.

Situation 3 You and your partner are about to retire and want to celebrate with a special holiday.

2 Now you are the sales consultant and your partner is the customer. Suggest alternatives from the box for the situation the customer describes. Finish by recommending the best option.

Situation 4	A tour of Northern India including a visit to the Taj Mahal A week in a luxury spa An eight-day cruise around the Mediterranean [Your own suggestion]
Situation 5	A self-drive tour in a motor home A Greyhound Coach Canada Pass A pass for the Trans-Canadian railway [Your own suggestion]
Situation 6	An apartment in a Mediterranean resort A trip to Disneyland A holiday in a family resort village like CenterParcs [Your own suggestion]

Unit 5 p.39

Investigating a client's needs

Customers

1 Students B & C
You and your partner are customers.
You are interested in an adventure holiday in South America.
You are not sure exactly where you want to go – perhaps Peru, Chile, or Argentina.
You would like some time for independent travel.
You would like to see some of the famous historical monuments as well, like Machu Picchu in Peru.
You've got three weeks in August.
You'll be travelling with five other friends in a group.
You don't want to spend very much money.
You want to fly direct to South America – you don't want to change planes anywhere outside Europe.

2 Students C & A
You and your partner are customers.
You are interested in a weekend break in a European city but you want something different – you've been to Paris, Rome, Madrid, etc. already.
You are not sure exactly where you want to go – perhaps one of the Baltic capitals (Tallinn, Riga, or Vilnius) or perhaps Warsaw or Berlin. You are not really sure.
You would like a tour with guided excursions and visits.
You want free time to do some shopping.
You don't really want to spend the whole time looking at monuments.
You've got four days any time in the spring.
You'll be travelling with a friend.
You want half-board and you want a bit of luxury – it's a special occasion.

3 Students A & B
You and your partner are customers.
You are interested in a beach holiday in Greece.
You'd like to see Athens and a bit of history, monuments – that sort of thing – but you are really interested in relaxing on the beach on an island.
You would quite like to do a bit of snorkelling or even try scuba diving, but nothing strenuous like walking.
You've got two weeks.
You want to try local food.
You want a villa or apartment so that you can do your own cooking.
You'll be travelling with a friend.
You want to hire a car and see the island.

Unit 8 p.71

Do you SWOT?

Student B

transport and access – excellent for both domestic and international arrivals (S)

accommodation – abundant but expensive and not very good (W)

restaurants, etc. – varied, good food, interesting (S)

local food – world-famous (S)

nightlife and clubbing – really good but only local people know about it (O)

museums and art galleries – not very attractive and often closed (W)

activities for families – there aren't many (W)

the weather – much too hot in summer. Rains all winter. (T)

marketing potential – quite limited because most tourists already know the city (T)

marketing strategy – a group of experts are preparing a new strategy (O)

current advertising – the city only uses a limited number of promotional techniques (O)

the image of the city – is often closely linked to other cities in the area (T)

Unit 4 p.35

Changes in tourist motivation

Student B

Survey B: What were the main reasons for your holiday journey?

1 Going to places I haven't visited before
2 Meeting new and different people
3 Opportunities to increase one's knowledge
4 Experiencing new and different lifestyles
5 Having fun, being entertained
6 Just relaxing
7 Escaping from the ordinary
8 Being together as a family
9 Trying new food
10 Talking about the trip after I returned home

Unit 10 p.90

Escape and enlightenment holidays

Student B

Camino de Santiago

THE PILGRIMAGE ROUTE OF ST JAMES

Probably the most famous Christian pilgrimage route of all is the medieval route to Santiago de Compostela in northern Spain, burial place of St James. Pilgrimages began in the 10th century.

We follow the whole route from Le Puy to Santiago in ten stages. You can choose the section that passes through the part of the country that interests you, and you can start at any point along the route.

Your luggage is moved ahead each day, and you are accommodated in comfortable small hotels and guest houses with breakfast and dinner unless otherwise stated.

Depart any day you like from 1 May to 30 October.

Unit 10 p.88

Questions on Antarctica

Student B

Answer A's questions using this information. Give as much detail as possible.

ANTARCTICA

Peninsula voyages generally depart from Ushuaïa in Argentina. Other South American ports are occasionally used.

For trips to the Ross region and Eastern Antarctica, commonly used ports are Hobart in Australia, and Auckland in New Zealand.

Departures sometimes set out from Cape Town and Port Elizabeth in South Africa, and Fremantle / Perth in Australia.

One of the main rules that will affect your visit is that only 100 passengers at any one time may be landed in any one place in Antarctica. This is to help preserve the fragile ecosystem. If you are on a small ship of up to 100 passengers, then you get a chance to go ashore every time. If the ship is larger, then there will be less opportunity for landings.

Ask A these questions. Make notes and ask for clarification and more details if necessary.

1 Do we need a visa?
2 What are the ships like?

Unit 7 p.62

Giving information about hotels

Student B

Unit 9 p.79

The air travel route map

Team B

Air ticket: A contract between an air carrier and a passenger that gives the passenger the right to travel on specific flights

Carrier code: A unique two-letter code that is used to identify an airline in official schedules and timetables. BA, for example, is the carrier code for British Airways

Code sharing: An agreement between two air carriers that allows the first carrier to use its carrier code on an aircraft operated by the second one

First class: The best service and highest fare offered by an airline

Frequent flyer program: A programme offered by airlines that gives frequent travellers points that are valid for free or discounted travel in the future

Gateway airport: An airport that is the main entry point to a particular region or country

Overbooking: The strategy airlines use of selling more seats than are available on the plane

RTW trip: An air ticket that allows a passenger to go round the world, stopping in at least three continents, but always travelling either east or west

Scheduled airline: An airline that offers regular flights that depart and arrive at published times

Transit: Passengers who are waiting to changes planes at a hub airport

Home	Hotels	Booking	Maps

InterCity Hotel Frankfurt ★★★

This modern hotel in the city centre, styled for the international business traveller's needs, is within walking distance of the city's busy fairground and the financial district with its characteristic skyscrapers, and offers guests free use of all Frankfurt public transport, including the return trip to the airport.

HOTEL FACILITIES

General Services
- Dry Cleaning / Laundry Service
- 24-Hour Front Desk
- Safety Deposit Boxes
- Left Luggage / Storage Facilities
- Cots / Cribs
- Restaurant
- Lounge / Bar

Business Facilities
- Meeting Facilities
- Secretarial Services
- Internet Access
- Black & White Photocopying
- Fax Service
- TV & Video Hire

Unit 10 p.90

Escape and enlightenment holidays

Student C

Dhanakosa Buddhist Retreat

Yoga and Meditation

Dhanakosa is a Buddhist Meditation, and Yoga retreat centre in Scotland, an ideal place for learning meditation and complementary activities like yoga, t'ai chi, hiking, and shiatsu. Dhanakosa sits by the shores of Loch Viol and is surrounded by the magnificent mountains and forests of the Scottish Highlands. It provides a quiet and beautiful setting for retreats.

Retreats are an ideal situation in which to take a fresh look at yourself and your life. You can learn to meditate or take your meditation further with the help of experienced teachers. This can help you develop clarity, confidence, energy, and positive emotion. These retreats provide an excellent introduction to both meditation and Buddhism.

Yoga and meditation: In these retreats the yoga work is presented as an important part of meditation practice. The classes are taught from basic principles and can be enjoyed by people with any level of experience.

Book early as these retreats are very popular.

Unit 1 p.8

Job skills

Student B

Information	Jamyang Shiwah	Maria Sanchez
Nationality		Mexican
Age		25
Job		Children's activity organizer in Cancun, Mexico
Qualities and skills		Friendly and patient Good with children
Working hours		8.00 to 12.00 and 16.00 to 20.00
Typical daily tasks		Organizes games and activities; takes children on trips; supervises meal times; babysitting
Things he / she enjoys about the job		Working with children, being in a holiday resort
Relaxing after work		Reading or sleeping, sometimes dancing
Own holidays		Visits friends in Mexico and the US

Grammar reference

1 Modal verbs, Verbs + -*ing* form or the infinitive, Present Simple and Present Continuous

Modal verbs

Modal verbs are special verbs that we use to talk about necessity, obligation, ability, and possibility. The most common are: *have to, need to, must, can, could, may, might, should*, and *ought to*.

Modal verbs are followed by the infinitive. With the exception of *have to* and *need to*, they are not formed in the same way as ordinary verbs.

Positive

I / You / He / She / It / We / They	**can start** work immediately.

= subject + ***can*** + infinitive

NOT *He can ~~to~~ start work immediately.*

Negative

I / You / He / She / It / We / They	**cannot (can't) start** work immediately.

= subject + ***can't*** + infinitive

NOT *I ~~don't can~~ start work immediately.*

Questions

Can	I / you / he / she / it / we / they	**start** work immediately?

= ***Can*** + subject + infinitive

NOT ~~*Do you can*~~ *start work immediately?*

The negative forms of other modals are *must not* (*mustn't*), *could not* (*couldn't*), *may not, might not* (*mightn't*), *should not* (*shouldn't*), and *ought not to* (*oughtn't to*).

Have to and *need to* are formed in the same way as the verbs *have* and *need*.

*She **has to** be flexible.*
*We **don't have to** work long hours.*
*Do I **need to** wear a uniform?*

Verbs + -*ing* form or the infinitive

Some verbs and expressions are followed by the -*ing* form or a noun. These include *be good at, dislike, enjoy, feel confident about, like*.

*I **am good at making** people relax.*

Other verbs and expressions are followed by the infinitive. These include *be able to, be willing to, can, have to* (= it is necessary to), *know how to*.

*We **are willing to work** long hours.*

Note that some verbs can be followed by *to* + infinitive or -*ing* form, with no change in meaning. These include: *begin, continue, dislike, intend, like, love, prefer, start*.

*She **likes working** independently.*
*She **likes to work** independently.*

Present Simple

Positive

I / You / We / They	**provide**	good service.
He / She / It	**provides**	good service.

= subject + infinitive

Negative

I / You / We / They	**do not (don't)**	**understand** the language.
He / She / It	**does not (doesn't)**	**understand** the language.

= subject + ***do / does*** + ***not*** + infinitive

Questions

Do	I / you / we / they	**have** a private bathroom?
Does	he / she / it	**have** a private bathroom?

= ***Do / Does*** + subject + infinitive

Be careful with the *he / she / it* forms.

NOT *He ~~provide~~ good service.*
NOT *She ~~don't~~ understand the language.*

We use the Present Simple to talk about things that are always true.

*A tour operator **organizes** the different parts of a holiday.*

We can use the Present Simple + an adverb of frequency to talk about habitual actions in the present.

*I **usually finish** work at 5 p.m.*

To talk about a temporary activity or arrangement in the present we use the Present Continuous.

Present Continuous

Positive

I	am	working.
You / We / They	are	working.
He / She / It	is	working.

= subject + *am / is / are* + *-ing* form

Negative

I	am not ('m not)	working.
You / We / They	are not (aren't)	working.
He / She/ It	is not (isn't)	working.

= subject + *am / is / are* + *not* + *-ing* form

Questions

Am	I	working?
Are	you / we / they	working?
Is	he / she / it	working?

= *Am / Is / Are* + subject + *-ing* form

There are some verbs which cannot be used in the Present Continuous. These are *have* (= possess), and thinking and feeling verbs such as *dislike, hate, know, like, love, remember, want.*

*I **hate** my new job.*
NOT *I'm hating my new job.*

2 Describing features and resources, Present Simple Passive

Describing features and resources

We often use the Present Simple to describe features and resources.

*New Zealand **lies** in the South Pacific Ocean.*
*It **consists** of two islands.*

*The islands **are** very green. **There are** many beautiful flowers.*
*The extreme north **has got** a subtropical climate.*

Note: *consist + of + noun.*

Remember that we use *There is* + singular or uncountable nouns and *There are* + plural nouns.

When describing a location we can use verbs such as *be* or *lie.* However, it is also very common to use the Present Simple Passive.

Present Simple Passive

Positive

New Zealand	**is located**	in the South Pacific Ocean.

= subject + *am / is / are* + past participle

Negative

New Zealand	**is not (isn't) located**	in the South Pacific Ocean.

= subject + *am / is / are* + *not* + past participle

Questions

Is New Zealand	**located**	in the South Pacific Ocean?

= *Am / Is / Are* + subject + past participle

*It **consists** of two islands.*
NOT *It is consisted of two islands.*
*The Balearic Islands **are located** between Spain and North Africa.*
NOT *The Balearic Islands locate between Spain and North Africa.*

Other verbs like *be located* are *be situated* and *be found.*
*Mount Etna **is found** in Sicily.*
*The main harbour **is situated** on the west coast.*

The verbs *lie, consist,* and *have got* are not used in the Passive.

3 Present Simple questions, Prepositions of time

Questions

We usually make Present Simple questions with *do / does.*

Do	you	**have**	a brochure?

= *Do / Does* + subject + infinitive.

We usually answer *Yes* or *No* to these questions.

With some verbs, questions are not formed with *Do / Does*. These include the verbs *be, can,* and *have got*.

Is	the hotel	near the sea?

= Present Simple of ***be*** + subject

Can	you	**give**	me a discount?

= ***Can*** + subject + infinitive

Have	you	**got**	a brochure?

= Present Simple of ***have*** + subject + ***got***

Note that it is possible to say both *Do you have?* and *Have you got?*

Question words

Sometimes we begin a question with a question word when we want specific information. The most common are: *who, what, which, where, when, how,* and *why*.

When *does the tour begin?*
How *can I help you?*

What and *which* can be followed by a noun.

What class *of hotel do you use?*

Other question words are *how much, how many, how often, how soon, how far,* and *how long*.

How much *does the tour cost?*

Prepositions of time

We often use the prepositions *in, at, on,* and *for* to talk about time.

in parts of days, months, seasons, years
in *the morning,* **in** *the afternoon*
in *March*
in *winter*
in *2007*
to say how soon something is going to happen
The tour will start **in** *two weeks.*

at times of the day, mealtimes
at *8 a.m.,* **at** *4 p.m.*
at *midnight,* **at** *dawn*
at *breakfast,* **at** *lunch*
also: **at** *night,* **at** *the weekend,* **at** *Easter*

on days of the week, special days, dates
on *Sunday,* **on** *Saturday afternoon*
on *Christmas Eve,* **on** *my birthday*
on *7 June*

for to talk about how long something will last
We will stay in Barcelona **for** *two days /* **for** *a long time /* **for** *a short time.*

4 Giving reasons, describing trends

Reasons

There are several ways of giving a reason for something: *because, because of, to, for, in case*.

I'm in London **because** *I'm going to a university reunion.*
because + subject + verb

The flight was delayed **because of** *fog.*
because of + noun

We went to Berlin **for** *my sister's wedding.*
for + noun

They're in New York **to** *attend a conference.*
to + infinitive

In case refers to a reason that might happen.
We're leaving early **in case** *there are delays.*
(= because there might be delays)

These expressions are often used in response to the following types of questions.

Why *are you travelling to Madrid?*
What's the reason for *the delay?*
What's the purpose of *the supplement?*

Describing trends

We can describe current and past trends by using different tenses.

Present Continuous describes a current trend.

People	**are taking**	more diverse holidays.

= subject + ***is / are*** + ***-ing***

Present Perfect describes a trend that began in the past and which continues up to the present.

Independent holidays	**have become**	more popular.

= subject + ***has / have*** + **past participle**

Past Simple describes a trend that ended in the past.

The country's revenue from tourism	**increased**.

= subject + **past form**

It is common to use a time phrase with the different tenses to show what period of time we are referring to. These often go at the beginning of the sentence.

Present Continuous   *nowadays, today*

Present Perfect   *since* + past point in time, *so far, up to now*

Past Simple   dates, periods of time in the past

Nowadays, *fewer people are using travel agents.*
Since 1999, *the number of holidays booked online has increased each year.*
Between 1985 and 1998, *Spain's revenue from package tourism dropped.*

Adverbs of degree

We often use an adverb of degree to show how quickly or slowly trends develop. These include:

slowly / gradually / steadily ➡ *strongly / sharply / dramatically*

Online bookings have increased **dramatically** *over the past five years.*

5 Open and closed questions, Suggestions and advice

Questions

Closed questions can be replied to with *yes* or *no*. They generally begin with a form of the verb *be* or an auxiliary verb such as *do, can,* or *have*.

Can she **stay** for longer than two weeks?	Yes, she can. / No, she can't.
Do you often **go** on package holidays?	Yes, I do. / No, I don't.

= **auxiliary verb** + subject + **main verb**

Note that it is more usual in English to reply to a closed question with a short answer, rather than a simple *yes* or *no*.

Open questions are used when we want information. They begin with question words such as *where, who, what, which, when, why, whose, how*. Other question words beginning with *how* are:

how long (= time)
how far (= distance)
how often (= frequency)
how much / many (= quantity)

How did you travel here?	By train. / I travelled here by train.
When did you arrive?	At 10 o'clock. / I arrived at 10 o'clock.

= **question word** + *did* + main verb

Suggestions and advice

There are several ways of making suggestions and offering advice.

You should	+ infinitive	***You should*** *try the Best of Australia tour.*
Why don't you	+ infinitive	***Why don't you*** *take the full-board option?*
You could	+ infinitive	***You could*** *look for information on the Internet.*
If I were you, I'd	+ infinitive	***If I were you, I'd*** *travel in the spring.*
Your best option is to	+ infinitive	***Your best option is to*** *hire a car.*
How about	+ -ing	***How about*** *going by bus?*
Have you thought about	+ -ing	***Have you thought about*** *going by bus?*

6 Comparatives, Describing a timetable

Comparatives

When we are comparing two things, we use the comparative form. Look at the table below.

Adjective type	Ending	Example
One syllable	+ *-er*	*cheap cheaper*
One syllable ending in *-e*	+ *-r*	*large larger*
One syllable ending in one vowel + one consonant	duplicate consonant + *-er*	*big bigger*

Note: we do not duplicate *w*.

Two syllables ending in *y*	replace *y* with *i* + *er*	*easy* *easier*
Two or more syllables	+ *more* + adjective	*comfortable* *more comfortable*
Irregular adjectives		*good* *better* *bad* *worse* *far* *farther* OR *further*

Other ways of making comparisons are

(not) as … as   *A bus is **not as** convenient **as** a taxi.*

less + adjective + *than*   *The trains are **less frequent** now **than** in the morning.*

Describing a timetable

The simplest way of describing a timetable is to use the Present Simple and a time or place phrase.

The train	**departs**	at 9.00.

= subject + **Present Simple** + phrase

A phrase can consist of

a preposition of time, e.g., *at midnight, in the morning, on Tuesdays*
a preposition of place, e.g., *from platform one, in the main square, at the bus stop.*

We use verbs such as *leave, depart, arrive, run, operate, take.*
*The ferry **takes** one hour and thirty minutes.*

To describe special rules or instructions on timetables, a passive form is often used, e.g. *may / can / may not / must / must not* + *be* + past participle
*Baggage **must not be left** unattended.*

7 Describing location

We use certain prepositions to describe where things and people are. These include *at, in, on, between, near (to),* and *next to.*

at   for a building or an address
*Many people stay **at** our campsite.*
*The guest house is located **at** 12 Northumberland Avenue.*

in   for a specific street, town, or country, and the countryside in general
*The hotel is **in** Northumberland Avenue.*
*I'd prefer to stay somewhere **in** the countryside.*

on   for rivers, the coast, famous streets, and floors of a building
*I'm staying at a hotel **on** Fifth Avenue.*
*Our room is **on** the seventh floor.*

Note that both *in* and *at* can be used for buildings. *In* generally refers to a position inside, while *at* suggests the function of the building.

*He's **at** the gym.* (= he is doing exercise)
*He's **in** the gym.* (= his location is inside the gym)

In, at, and *on* are used in many other expressions to describe location, which need to be learnt individually, e.g. **in** *the middle,* **at** *home,* **on** *the top.*

Between means in the middle of two things.
*The gymnasium is **between** the car park and the swimming pool.*

Opposite means on the other side to a person, building, or other object.

*My hotel is **opposite** the station.*
NOT *My hotel is ~~opposite to~~ the station.*

Near (to) means not very far from something or someone.

*I'd prefer to be **near (to)** the financial district.*

Next to means at the side of something or someone.

*I am standing **next to** the conference centre.*

8 Verb patterns, Superlatives

Verb patterns

There are several types of verb patterns:

verb + object *provide, offer*	*The hotel **provided a questionnaire** for each guest.*
verb + *to* + infinitive *be prepared to,* *hope to, need to*	*The company **is prepared to invest** heavily.* *We are **hoping to attract** a lot more customers.* *The hotel **needs to develop** a leisure programme.*
verb + object + *to* + infinitive *give, send, ask, tell*	*We **asked him to write** a report.*
verb + object + infinitive *let, make*	***Let your customers know** about changes to your services.* ***The hotel made him pay** a single supplement.*

Superlatives

When we are comparing more than two things, we use the superlative form. Compare the rules for formation of the comparative and the superlative.

Adjective type	Ending	Example
One syllable	+ -**est**	*cheap* *the cheap**est***
One syllable ending in *-e*	+ -**st**	*large* *the larg**est***
One syllable ending in one vowel + one consonant	duplicate consonant + -**est**	*big* *the big**gest***
Note: we do not duplicate *w*.		
Two syllables ending in *y*	replace *y* with *i* + -**est**	*easy* *the easi**est***
Two or more syllables	**the most** + adjective	*famous* ***the most** famous*

Irregular adjectives	*good*
	the best
	bad
	the worst
	far
	the farthest OR
	the furthest

*Italy's tourism campaign was judged to be **the best**.*
***The highest** number of people voted for New York's campaign.*
*All the campaigns highlighted **the most interesting** and unusual aspects of the country.*

In the same way that *less* is the opposite of *more*, *most* is the opposite of *least*.

***The least successful** campaign was also **the most innovative**.*

9 Like or dislike, Polite questions

Like or dislike

There are several ways of talking about things that we like or dislike.

Strongly like =	*really love* *love* *really like* *like* *prefer* *quite like*
Neutral =	*don't mind* *don't like / dislike* *really don't like* *hate*
Strongly dislike =	*really hate*

All these expressions take the same structure: verb + -*ing* or verb + noun.

*I **really hate queuing** at the check-in. / I **really hate** the check-in.*
*She **doesn't mind waiting** in the departure lounge.*
*Do you **like landing**?*

Note that *mind* can only take verb +-*ing*.

Polite questions

We usually make questions with an auxiliary verb and a main verb.

Can you **answer** a few questions?

= **auxiliary verb** + subject + **main verb**

Where **do** you **work**?

= question word + **auxiliary verb** + subject + **main verb**

We can make questions more polite by phrasing them in a less direct way.

Would you mind + -ing	***Would you mind telling** me what you do?*
Could you + infinitive	***Could you give** me a few minutes of your time?*
Can I ask you + indirect question	***Can I ask you** where you work?*

Note the difference between a direct and an indirect question.

Direct question

Where do you work?

= question word + auxiliary + subject + infinitive

Indirect question

(Can you tell me) where you work?

= question word + subject + infinitive

10 Talking about experience, Describing service provision

Talking about experience

We often use the Past Simple and the Present Perfect to talk about experience.

Past Simple

Positive

I **enjoyed** the tour.

= subject + past form

Negative

I **didn't see** the Northern Lights.

= subject + ***did not (didn't)*** + **infinitive**

Questions	Short answers
Did you **visit** the famous Ice Hotel?	Yes, I did. No, I didn't.

= ***Did*** + subject + **infinitive**

We use the Past Simple to talk about something that happened on a particular occasion in the past. We often use time expressions with the Past Simple.

*They **found** a much better travel company.*
*I **tried** windsurfing last year.*

Present Perfect

Positive

I **have tried** white-water rafting.

= subject + ***have / has*** + past participle

Negative

I **haven't found** a suitable company.

= subject + ***have / has not*** + past participle

Questions	Short answers
Have you **visited** the famous market?	Yes, I have. No, I haven't.

= ***Have / has*** + subject + past participle

We use the Present Perfect to talk about things that have happened to us at some point in our lives. It is generally not important when these happened because the Present Perfect focuses on the experience itself.

*I've **climbed** Costa Rica's highest peak.*

When talking about experiences, we often use *ever* with questions in the Present Perfect to mean 'at any time in your life'.

***Have you ever visited** Machu Picchu?*   *No, **I've never been** there.*

Describing service provision

We can use several tenses and verb forms to describe the services that are available to customers.

Present Simple

Verbs such as *offer* and *provide* are a better choice than *have*, while *boast* is often used in persuasive styles of text.

*New York **offers** a wide range of attractions to suit all tastes.*

*Costa Rica **boasts** fantastic wildlife.*

can

You can + infinitive describes a range of possibilities.
***You can** learn about the Hindu religion and see the last unspoilt place in the world.*

Present Simple Passive

We can use verbs such as *present*, *provide*, and *offer* in this form.
*Many opportunities **are provided** to learn about the important ecological work in the area.*

Imperative

This is another structure that is often used in persuasive texts, as it addresses the reader directly.
***Book** now for the thrill of a lifetime!*

11 *If* sentences

If sentences

We use *if* to describe actions or situations that are conditional on other events. The *if* clause describes the condition, while the main clause describes the action or consequence.
***If you require** a special diet, please **let us know**.*

We can talk about conditions in the past, present, or future.

Condition

If + Present Simple, Present Continuous, Present Perfect
***If you are travelling** alone, you may have to pay a surcharge for your room.*

Note that we don't use *will* after *if*.

NOT *If you ~~will~~ require a special diet, please let us know.*

Consequence

Present Simple, imperative, *can, will, may, might, must, should*
*If you decide to stay for longer than a month, we **will offer** a discount.*

It is not always necessary to begin the sentence with the *if* clause.

*We will offer a 50% refund **if** you cancel your holiday.*

Note that there is no comma between the two parts of the sentence when *if* is in the second part of the sentence.

12 Responses and orders

Responding politely to questions and requests

When responding politely to requests and questions, we often give expanded answers rather than simply saying *yes* or *no*.

*Could you help me? Yes, **of course**.*
*Do you know if the train is on time? Yes, **I think so**.*
*Has the plane left? Yes, **I'm afraid it has**.*

We often begin a refusal or other negative response with an apology.

*Do you know where the nearest chemist is? **No, sorry**. I don't know the area very well.*
*Have you got a pen? **No, I'm sorry**, I haven't.*
*Couldn't you upgrade me? **I'm afraid not**. The flight's full.*

Giving orders and stopping people doing something

Some orders are more direct, and therefore less polite. Some are indirect and therefore more polite. However, a lot will depend on the tone of voice used to give the order.

Imperative

The imperative takes the infinitive form. In the negative, *Do not* or *Don't* come before the infinitive. This is the most direct way of giving an order.

***Fasten** your seatbelts.*
***Don't smoke** in this area.*

Please + imperative

Please + imperative is more polite than the imperative on its own, but still rather official.

***Please take** your jacket **off**.*
***Don't use** your mobile, **please**.*

Can / Could you ... ? + infinitive

Can is relatively informal, and is often used with *please*, while *could* is generally more polite than *can*.

Can you wait *behind the yellow line (please)?*
Could you fill in *this form?*

I'm sorry / I'm afraid

It is polite to apologize when stopping someone from doing something.

I'm afraid *this is a non-smoking area.*
I'm sorry, *you can't take photographs here.*

If clause

An *if* clause can be used to ask someone to do something. *If* is often followed by the Present Simple or *could*. This is the most polite form of instruction.

If you could *just take a few moments to fill in this form.*

Listening scripts

Unit 1 Listening

Three jobs

1

I like the job. I like being the front line, the first point of contact. I think I'm quite good at dealing with people. I know how to smile, although sometimes on a bad day, it's hard. I guess the tasks I do are a bit routine if I'm honest – I check in arrivals, hand out room keys, process enquiries and reservations, that kind of thing. I work shifts, which can be a drag. I usually start at six in the morning, which is OK because I get off nice and early, but then occasionally I do the late turn and I don't finish till after midnight – this week I'm doing the late shift.

There's always something different going on. For example, we had a group from Japan arrive yesterday and they were so polite and nice and pleased to be here. They're visiting the Snoopy Museum in Santa Rosa today and were so excited about it. I'm waiting for them to come back, so I can see how they all got on.

2

I started here about two years ago. As the manager, I'm mainly in the back office. I don't deal directly with the public at the desk. On a typical day, I'm on the phone and the email most of the time. I start the day by checking my email, and that sets the agenda for the first part of the morning at least. I have to talk to local businesses, hotels, tour companies, to check that we're providing the service they want, that we're stocking their brochures and so on. I also arrange presentations, and I get invited to a lot of social events to network and talk about tourism information services in the city. I'm working on a big presentation for some Italian clients at the moment.

3

This is my second season. A lot of reps only survive one season, because it's very demanding work – we don't get paid a lot and we only get one day off a week. I feel a lot more confident about things this time. I couldn't do the job all year, but as the season only lasts three months, it's OK. We work very long hours, especially on changeover days. We take the guests who are going home to the airport at six in the morning, and bring back the new group. We then have to get them settled, sort out any problems – and there always are problems! – and do the paperwork. So I often don't finish until midnight on changeover day.

I like working with people and on the whole the guests are good, but some of them can be very annoying – although I never show it of course, because the customer is always right!

Unit 1 Pronunciation

agent	guide	pilot
attendant	porter	attractions
manager	tourism	calm
catering		

Unit 2 Pronunciation

Russia	London	China
Madrid	Italy	Japan
France	Mexico	
Paris	Tokyo	

Unit 2 Listening

Where do tourists go?

Exercise 3

a We had a total of 19,000 visitors last year.
b The population is 80 million.
c The average age of visitors to the museum is 30.5 years.
d It takes about 15 minutes to get to the airport.

Exercise 4

19 90 18 80 13 30 15 50

Exercise 6

OK, I'm going to tell you the top ten tourist destinations in the world. The top country is a European country – can you guess which? To make it more interesting for you I'm going to start at the bottom with the tenth place, where we have Germany, which had a total of 19 million tourist visitors last year. In ninth place, we have Canada which had 20 million visitors. Then there are two countries together in seventh place: Mexico and Russia, both with 21 million. In sixth place comes the United Kingdom with 25 million visitors. Then in fifth place, and the highest Asian country – any ideas which one? (Japan?) No, not Japan. It's China with 31 million. In fourth place, we have Italy: 41 million; third is Spain with 48 million. Which leaves the top two: the United States in the silver medal position, if you like, with 51 million. And top of the charts, by a long way, is ... France with 75 million tourist visitors. Did anyone guess right?

Unit 2 Listening

Favourite places

I=Interviewer, L=Liz, R=Regula, V=Valery

I Liz, how do you like to spend your holidays?
L Well, I'm a teacher in London and I think because I work with people all the time, I just want to escape when I'm on holiday. So, most years I rent a remote cottage in the Borders, just inside Scotland. It's a long way from anywhere. It's got spectacular views, but the only building you can see is an old ruined castle, and that's five miles away.
I So what do you do there?
L Lots of walking through the hills. Or sometimes I drive over to the east where you've got the dramatic coastline of Northumberland. It's still unspoilt. No one can get hold of me. The cottage doesn't even have electricity, so there's no phone, no TV, and the mobile doesn't get reception, unless you climb the hill at the back of the cottage, but that's 600 metres – so it's got to be a real emergency!
I Sounds great. What about you, Regula – what's your favourite destination?
R I suppose you could say that Andreas – that's my boyfriend – and I collect cities. These days with cheap flights, it's almost cheaper than staying in Zurich. We go away for long weekends about five or six times a year. We've been to Vienna, Budapest, and Prague this year already. I love art galleries and walking through the streets of the ancient city. You get a feel for the cultural heritage of a place. But my favourite place at the moment has got to be Barcelona. I love the Gaudí architecture, and of course the delicious food. I think it's the complete city. It's also the place where Andreas and I went for our first holiday, so it's got happy memories for us.
I And finally, Valery. Where do you spend your holidays?
V Usually, I go to the Mediterranean. My father has a villa on Cyprus – my parents go there for a relaxing break, but it's not so interesting for me. I like to go to clubs with my friends, meet girls, dance, and drink a few beers. I think the best place is Ibiza. I've been there for two summers and it's a good scene with exciting nightlife and lively bars. I don't go for the sun. I think there are too many crowded beaches. Last year, I stayed on for the season since I got a job in a bar. That was cool! Maybe I'll go back this summer.
I Thanks everyone.

Unit 3 Listening

Why choose a package holiday?

I=Interviewer, H=Helga

I Helga, what would you say were the advantages of a package holiday?
H Well, I think the most obvious advantage

is the saving in cost. Package holidays are cheaper than the same holiday bought independently. We're tour operators, and so we're buying in bulk, and we buy in advance – sometimes as much as two years in advance – and this means that we get good prices for airline seats, for hotel rooms, for accommodation in general, and for other services. The independent traveller simply cannot get prices as good as ours. So yes, I'd say the low cost is the most important advantage.

I Are there any other advantages?

H Well, yes, there are. Another important advantage of the package holiday is that you know how much the holiday will cost before you've left home. The accommodation, transport, transfers, a lot of excursions – all this is included in the price. In fact, we call it an all-inclusive price – the only other money you will spend is buying souvenirs, drinks, or small things like that. With a family, where the money they have might be limited, you know how much the holiday's going to cost you before you leave home.

I Can you give me one more reason for taking a package holiday?

H Well, another thing is the fact that it's been organized by professionals. So, as tour operators we've been to the destination. We've confirmed that the hotel meets our standards and we've checked with local guides.

I So this means that you won't have any problems – you can relax, and …

H Yes, you're on holiday with nothing to worry about. And if you do have a problem, there's a rep, a representative of our company, on site. So if you have any problems, there's somebody who speaks your language that you can go to and this person will find a solution to your problem. And this also produces peace of mind.

Unit 3 Listening

The 'Peace in Burma' tour

I=Interviewer, B=Begoña

I What are the features of Burma that interest people from Europe?

B It's very peaceful. That's an important feature. Burma doesn't have a lot of tourists compared to Vietnam, Cambodia, especially compared to Thailand.

I What else does Burma offer?

B There are very good beaches and we are starting to have very good hotels also.

I Is it mainly beach tourism, or are there cultural attractions that people are going to Burma to see?

B Well, cultural attractions are the most common reason for visiting Burma.

I Can you give us details of what sort of things people see?

B Yes. We always start with Yangon or Rangoon, which is the capital of Burma. We stay there overnight the first night and the last night, when we enter and leave the country. And we always visit Bagan. Bagan is full of temples. It has more than 2,000 temples so our groups always stay there three nights, and they get to see a lot of the temples. Also they can rent a bicycle, they can go by horse-drawn carriage and it's a very interesting place. You can go down the river in Bagan too, and that's very nice.

I Where do you go after Bagan?

B After Bagan the second place we go to is Lake Inle, which is also amazing. We do a lot of trekking by Inle and also in the mountains, which are about one hour away by car. And we go to the floating markets there – people always like that. And then we move to Mandalay, which is in the middle of the country and is very traditional. And we go to the school of Buddhism, also in Mandalay.

I Wow. That sounds interesting!

B Yes, Mandalay's lovely. And then we move to the beach. We use Ngapali beach. We have to fly from Yangon or Mandalay to Thandwe, and then to Ngapali. We stay there two nights, and the beach is very, very beautiful.

I Is it difficult to persuade people to go to Burma?

B A little. The thing is that we find that people don't know anything about Burma. They are very scared, so we try to teach them, we try to tell them where it is located, that it's a very safe place, and we are like teachers with them, because they don't know what it is.

Unit 3 Pronunciation

Exercise 2

accept   agent   local   travel

Exercise 3

brochure	discount	inclusive
commission	domestic	package
component	holiday	providers
customer	include	transfers

Unit 4 Listening

Reasons for travel and money spent on travel

For British tourists, like most countries, leisure tourism is the main reason for travel with 53% travelling for this reason. Visiting friends and relatives, VFR, is the next biggest reason with 32%. Business tourism is relatively small at 11%.

When we look at the money spent on travel by British tourists, the order is slightly different. Leisure tourism accounts for 70% of expenditure, then business travel at 16%. Tourists and travellers who are visiting friends and relatives, not surprisingly perhaps, spend less money and this is only 11%.

Unit 4 Listening

Passenger survey

1

A Can I ask you a few questions?

B Certainly.

A We're collecting information to help us monitor passenger movements.

B OK.

A Can I ask where you are from?

B We're from Pakistan.

A And where are you going?

B To Mecca.

A Is that for a pilgrimage?

B That's right. We're going there to visit the Holy Shrine of the Prophet Mohammed. I've been to Mecca many times, but this is the first time for my family, so we are very excited.

A I see. And how long are you planning to stay?

B We'll probably stay for a week or so, because we want to do some sightseeing as well afterwards.

A OK, thanks very much. I hope it goes well.

B Thank you.

2

A Hello, madam. We're doing a passenger survey to help with tourism planning. I wonder if I could ask you some questions?

C All right.

A Where are you travelling to?

C Bangkok, Thailand. One moment please … No, it's nothing. Sorry about that. I have to have the phone on in case there's a problem at the office.

A No problem … What is the purpose of your visit? Are you travelling for a business trip?

C Yes, I suppose so, but it's, well, yes, it's also pleasure too, at least I hope so. It's a fam trip – a familiarization trip. I'm a tour operator, part of a group of tour operators from Italy. We're being taken out to Thailand because we need to see what the facilities will be like for our tourists. We want to start a new tour programme there for the Italian market.

A How long is the trip?

C Five days.
A Great. Thank you, and good luck.

3
A Excuse me, have you got time to answer a few quick questions?
D I think so.
A Can I start by asking where you've travelled from this morning and where you're going to?
D I'm from London and I drove here this morning. I'm off to New York.
A And what's the reason for your trip?
D It's my brother's wedding and I'm his best man!
A A very important job. Does he live in New York?
D Yes, he went there a few years ago to start a software company – he's been very successful.
A How long are you staying?
D Well, probably four days, but I've got an open return in case they ask me to stay on for a bit longer. You never know … was that the New York flight they just called?
A I'm not sure. Why don't you check? I haven't got any more questions.
D OK, thanks!

4
A Can I ask you some questions for a survey we're doing?
E Yes, of course.
A Have you just come in on the Madrid flight?
E Yes, but we started in Buenos Aires. We are from Argentina, but we had to fly to Madrid because there were no direct flights available.
A Where are you going to?
E To London.
A Why are you visiting London?
E We are going to London for a study tour for four weeks. We are learning English.
A Apart from learning English, do you have any other reasons to be here, any other things you want to do?
E Yes, we have a lot of day trips and excursions to famous places, and we want to go to Scotland to see the Edinburgh festival. We want to do sightseeing, but not just sightseeing, we are here because we want to know about the culture, and not only because of the famous sights.

Unit 4 Pronunciation

Exercise 1
Russia   China   Germany

Exercise 3
brochure	destination	package
change	English	passenger
chart	Egypt	pilgrimage
check-in	expression	religious
cultural	language	

Unit 4 Listening

Interview with a Kenyan tour operator

I=Interviewer, J=John Muhoho

I John, tell us a little about yourself and how you started working in tourism.
J I'm 39 years old. I started working in tourism in 1994, after finishing a degree in Geography and Political Science at the University of Nairobi. I started my company, CKC Tours in 2000 with some friends.
I What do you enjoy most about the job?
J Meeting as many different people as possible. I'm able to understand them, I'm able to understand their culture, and of course I'm able to get some money!
I Do you get people from all over the world?
J Yes, I get people right now because of the Internet. Our site is able to generate business because we have registered with several search engines, like Google and Yahoo. It's able to give us business from all over the world.
I Does most of your business come through the Internet?
J Not exactly, but a good portion of it – maybe 25%.
I In Kenya, is tourism regarded as a good industry to work in?
J Yes, it's the biggest. It's a very important industry.
I So, why should I come to Kenya?
J Kenya offers a diverse range of interests for visitors. We have 300 kilometres of coast, with some lovely long beaches. There are coral reefs, and swimming in the sea is safe from sharks and sea creatures. That's one side, that's the beach holiday. Then Kenya is famous for safaris. There are 45 national parks, where clients can come and visit and see exotic animals like flamingos – there are about two million of them. You can also go hiking in the hills and mountains. There is the culture aspect, such as the Masai, who are not very exposed to Western civilization. Basically, that's the safari and beach side. You can also come for golf. We have 39 golf courses, so you can integrate a golfing holiday – safari, beach, golf. We also have some camels, where people can just go for a camel ride. In a nutshell, I can say that Kenya is a wonderful place for visitors to come. Kenyan people are very friendly people.

Unit 5 Listening

All in a day's work

1
Hi. I'm taking a year off when I finish my studies and I want to go around the world. I'm told there are round-the-world tickets, and I wanted a bit of information about them.

2
Could you book me a double somewhere central in Helsinki for next weekend? Arrive Friday midday. Depart Monday morning. Oh, and non-smoking.

3
Hello. I wonder if you can help us. We want to go to Mexico to see the Aztec ruins, but we're a little nervous. We don't speak Spanish, you see. And at our age we don't want too much adventure.

4
Hi. Can you tell me what I need for Kazakhstan? Will I be OK with US dollars? And I suppose I need a visa?

5
Hi. We booked with you last week to go to Orlando – you know, Disney and all that. But we're just a bit worried about it. I mean if something happens while we're there. I'm not saying an accident, but anybody can fall ill.

Unit 5 Listening

A new customer

T=Travel agent, K=Karl, A=Anita

T Hello. Can I help you?
K Hello. Yes. We want to go to Australia.
T Australia? OK. Have a seat and we'll see what we can do.
A Thanks. Our daughter's there and we want to go out and do a bit of travelling with her.
T So, were you thinking about a package tour, perhaps?
K Well, we were, but the problem is that Nicki's already out there. I mean, there's not much point paying an airfare for her.
A We haven't really got a lot of money for this.
K We just want to travel around out there with her, you know.
T So you'd prefer to do things on your own? Be free to move around in your own time?
K Yes!
T You want something not too expensive …
K No.
T … but you want to book your flights and so on before you go?

K Yes, that's right. What do you think? What should we do?

T Well, probably your best option is to travel out to Australia independently, and then once you're there, take a tour run by a local tour operator. Where is your daughter, by the way?

A In Melbourne.

T Ah, that's great. There's loads you can do from there. And when exactly did you want to travel?

A Well, ideally on the 20th of July. We can't really go any earlier.

T And what about your stay? How long would you want to be away?

A Three weeks, we thought. It would be nice to stay longer, but …

T Three weeks is fine. Now, let's see. Your daughter's in Melbourne, you said?

K Yes, so we thought we'd spend a couple of days there at the beginning while we get used to the time difference.

T Good idea. It's a big difference. It's a bit of a shock for the body clock. So, let's see … it's Mr and Mrs …?

A Chodkiewicz.

T And have you booked with us before, by any chance?

A We haven't actually. We were passing and …

T That's no problem, Mrs Chodkiewicz. It was just to see if we had you on the computer. Now, what have we got that might interest you …

Unit 5 Listening

Presenting a product

T … what have we got that might interest you … Hmm, let's see … there are a couple of things that I can think of straight away. Of course, a lot depends on what you're interested in doing in Australia. Did you have anything in mind?

K I'd like to see Ayers Rock.

A I want to go to the Great Barrier Reef.

T Ah. They're quite a long way apart.

K Yes, we saw that – we were looking at the map. It's big!

T Not to worry. Melbourne is a good base, and if I can just show you this. This company specializes in independent tours and they have two in Australia that you should think about, in my opinion. One's called All Australia. That's nineteen days. It goes along the coast to Adelaide then by train to Ayers Rock. Then you fly to Darwin in the north, and then to Cairns. That means you both get to see what you want.

A Is everything included?

T Everything. The flights, the train, the

coaches when you go anywhere by road.

K And the hotels? And all the meals?

T The hotels … and you can take the full-board option with all the meals. But if I were you, I'd take half-board. Full-board is too much food for most people, and with half-board you have the fun of choosing where to have lunch each day.

A That's a good idea!

K Nineteen days did you say?

T That's right.

K Hmm. It's a bit long, perhaps. It doesn't leave much time in Melbourne.

A No.

T Well then, why don't you think about the Australia's Best tour? That's only thirteen days. Here we are. It's like the last one but you go direct from Melbourne to Alice Springs.

A That's where you go to Ayers Rock?

T That's right.

K And it goes to the Great Barrier Reef?

T And Sydney. And as I said, it's only thirteen days so you'll have more time in Melbourne.

K This is harder than I thought.

A Yes, it's complicated.

T Look, why don't you leave your contact details with me and I'll have a look on the Internet and in our brochures, and see if I can find anything else for you. Then if you can come in some time next week …

K OK.

T Could you give me your name so I can set up a file for you?

A Chodkiewicz. Anita Chodkiewicz.

T Could I ask you to spell that?

A Yes, it's C-H-O-D- …

T C-H-O-D- …

Unit 5 Pronunciation

A, B, C, D, E, F, G, H, I, J, K, L, M, N, O, P, Q, R, S, T, U, V, W, X, Y, Z

Unit 6 Pronunciation

Exercise 1

clean	jet	safe
easy	leisure	scenic
ferry	plane	train

Exercise 4

car	fast	harbour
craft	guard	ride
drive	guide	track

Unit 6 Listening

Transport systems and cable cars in San Francisco

Welcome to the San Francisco public transportation information line. San Francisco has a variety of transit options for visitors. For information on ferry crossings in the Bay Area, press 1. For information on MUNI buses and metro services, press 2. For information on the BART, Bay Area Rapid Transit train system, including services to San Francisco International airport, press 3. For information on the world-famous cable cars, press 4. For any other information, including bike rental, coach tours, and car rental, please hold for an operator.

You have chosen option 4. San Francisco's historic cable cars have been running since 1873. They provide an unusual and interesting way to see the city with stunning views. There are three lines: California–Van Ness, Powell–Mason, and Powell–Hyde. The cable cars run from 6 a.m. to 1 a.m, Monday through Sunday. At peak times they are approximately every five to ten minutes. Tickets can be bought at special booths or on the car at $3 for a single ride. Tickets are non-transferable. Special one-day and one-week passes are available. You can board at any of the stops indicated with the brown cable-car sign. Cable-car riders should hold on tight and take great care when getting on and off.

Unit 6 Listening

A cruise ship worker

I started out as a junior waiter in the restaurant of a four-star hotel. They gave me a thorough training in all aspects of waiting, including silver service – that's where you serve the diners at the table – which you need to know for jobs on cruise ships. I stayed there for about two years before moving to work in a French restaurant in Manchester where I was deputy head waiter.

I'd heard on the grapevine that jobs were available on cruise lines. So, I put together a letter explaining what I was looking for and a CV listing my work experience. I sent these off, with a photo, to some of the cruise lines and cruise line employment agencies. One of them accepted me after an interview and put me on their waiting list. Four months later, I was on my way to Miami to join the Crown Princess.

Our hours of work are quite long and we don't get a regular weekly day off. This ship cruises around the Caribbean but we don't get to go ashore at every port. We're not allowed to mix with the passengers off duty or use any passenger facilities. But we have got our own social facilities, all food and accommodation is free, and the social life on board is amazing.

Unit 7 Listening

A place to stay

1

Hi, I need a room for tonight … No, just myself … That's right. Just for tonight … You've only got doubles? No singles? … No, no. Non-smoking. … Mm, OK. I'll take it, I guess. Thank you very much.

2

Hello. Is that Sea View? … Do you have a room for two for tonight and tomorrow? … Yes, a double or a twin. Either would be perfect. Is the bathroom en-suite? … A washbasin and shower is fine … Oh, supper would be wonderful. That saves us going back out again … Davidson … Yes, OK. We'll see you this evening, then.

3

Hello. I've been looking at your website and I'm ringing to see if you would have a space for a family of five – that's my wife and me, and our children? … No, all in the same tent. It's a standard tent. A frame tent, I think you say … Electricity? No … no, we don't … No, actually … I mean, to tell you the truth, we'd like not to be near the shower block. As far away as possible in fact … For two weeks from July 22nd … A deposit of 15%? OK. How should I send that?

Unit 7 Listening

Taking a reservation by telephone

R=Receptionist, C=Caller

R The Hadrian Hotel, Sara speaking. Can I help you?
C Hi. Would you have a room for next week?
R For next week, madam? When would that be exactly?
C From the 12th to the 15th.
R And would that be a single room?
C No, it's for me and my daughter.
R Would you prefer a twin or two singles?
C A twin, please.
R Smoking or non-smoking?
C Non-smoking.
R So that's arriving Monday the 12th, departure Thursday the 15th, twin, non-smoking?
C That's right.
R One moment, please. I'll just check availability. Yes, we can do that. What name is it, please?
C Steinmetz. Barbara Steinmetz.
R Could you spell that, please?
C Yes, it's S-T-E-I-N-M-E-T-Z.
R … I-N-M-E-T-Z.
C That's right.
R We need you to confirm this, Ms Steinmetz. By fax or email. Or you can give us your credit card details.
C Credit card is easiest.
R Could you give me the number of the card?
C Just a moment … Yes, it's 49 double 2 6481 6262 double 3 83.
R So that's 49 double 2 6481 6262 double 3 83.
C Yes, that's it.
R Is that Visa, Ms Steinmetz?
C No, it's Mastercard.
R And what's the name on the card, please?
C My own name. It's my name.
R OK. And could you just tell me the expiry date?
C It expires August 2008.
R That's fine then, Ms Steinmetz. Your reservation number is H-A-D, 280, 6 double 5, double 03.
C … double 5, double 03.
R Could I ask you to use this if you need to modify or cancel your booking?
C Yes, of course.
R And we look forward to seeing you on the 12th. Thank you for calling.
C Thank you. Goodbye.
R Goodbye.

Unit 7 Pronunciation

Can I help you?
Would that be a single room?
Would you prefer a twin …
… or two singles?

Unit 8 Listening

Analysing your product

I=Interviewer, J=Jean

I Jean, what would you say the strengths of the NewcastleGateshead product are?
J I would say we have three main strengths, the strongest of which is the people that live here. They're very proud of their origins, and of the North-east, and they show it to the visitors. Another strength is the place because we're surrounded by wonderful countryside and areas that are very beautiful.
I And your third strength?
J A third strength is that we've also got two very vibrant cities. We've got the old parts of Newcastle – the castle and the area around Grey Street, and on the Gateshead side we've got some fabulous new attractions such as the Gateshead Millennium Bridge and the Baltic. An excellent product showing the old and the new together.
I And you've got the Sage, of course.
J We've got the new Sage Gateshead, which is a home to music, musical discovery, and education, too.
I OK, fantastic. How about opportunities for the city? For the cities!
J For the cities. Well, we call NewcastleGateshead a destination. Our airport has grown massively over the last eighteen months. That gives us many opportunities to speak to new markets, to bring people from outside the UK into NewcastleGateshead.
I A threat?
J We have a threat with regard to the perception that people have of the North-east. They see the area as quite an industrial place, which in reality it isn't at all, so we do have to change that perception.
I Right.
J So the perceptions in the UK, I would say is our main threat.
I A major weakness?
J A major weakness? Well, all the other cities in the UK, such as Bristol and Birmingham and Manchester, all these cities are using the same product concept, which is the vibrant European city. And it's all very much the same offer, so that's a major weakness.
I Any other weaknesses?
J Another weakness would be the number of hotel rooms we have. If you think about the city of Glasgow in Scotland, they've got fifteen thousand bedrooms in the city. We have just over five thousand, so it's very difficult because sometimes the hotels are full, so that's a difficult problem for us.
I But that's a weakness which is the result of so many people wanting to visit NewcastleGateshead, isn't it? I mean, it's a weakness because of your success in marketing, surely?
J Yes, it is really.
I Well, that's a nice weakness!

Unit 8 Listening

Promotion in tourism

I Jean, can you tell me about the connection between marketing and promotion?
J Well, promotion is one of the four Ps of what we call the marketing mix.
I The four Ps?
J Yes, the four Ps. Product, in other words, what you're offering. Price, which is how

much it's going to cost. Place, which is more about where you show the product to the client than about where the holiday itself actually happens. And number four, Promotion.

I Which is your area, if I'm not mistaken?

J That's right.

I So, tell us a little bit about promotions, then.

J Well, the idea of promotion is to sell your product. But the interesting part is, 'How do we do this?', and the answer begins with awareness, with making the customer aware that the product exists.

I So promotion is making customers aware?

J Yes, but it's also about creating a demand. And then of course, another use of promotion is to make customers understand that your product is better than other similar products.

I So we know why we use promotion, but how does promotion work? How do you create a demand, for example?

J Well, creating a demand is a question of promotional techniques.

I You mean advertising?

J Yes. Advertising is one of the things we do in promotion, but it's not the only technique. Apart from advertising – you know, magazines, TV, the media in general – there's also PR. That's short for Public Relations. This could be an article in a newspaper or magazine. An article is free publicity, though it's never really free!

I So we've got advertising and PR. Is there anything else?

J Yes, there's what we call direct marketing.

I You mean going straight to the customer?

J Yes. The provider – that could be a tour operator with a package holiday, or an airline with a special offer – the provider contacts the customer directly, usually by mailing information and news directly to the customers on their database.

I And is that emailing, or do you use normal post?

J A lot of small tour operators use email, but for most big companies, direct marketing is letters through your door.

I Any other promotional techniques?

J There's also personal selling. Now that does need an intermediary, because personal selling is a travel agent sitting with a client. And it's knowing who you spoke to last week and what they want. Personal selling's your smile. It's the human touch.

Unit 8 Pronunciation

advertise	improve	strengths
ancient	innovative	threats
campaign	marketing	weaknesses
identify	picturesque	

Unit 9 Take off

A typical flight? Well, for the passenger the whole process begins on arriving at the airport. Check-in first, and then you go through security control. After that it's a question of sitting around waiting for the flight to be called. Boarding next – which is the first time we come into contact with the passengers, although of course, we've been on board for a while by then. Last passenger on, doors shut, push off from the finger, and then we're taxiing towards the runway for take-off. A lot of people get nervous just before take-off, but it's over in seconds and suddenly we're up, we're in the air, we're flying. Speed 550 km an hour, cruising at 33,000 feet, way above the clouds. Wonderful.

Unit 9 Listening

The ups and downs of flying

1

I actually love travelling to the airport, driving to the airport, because it's usually that moment when you're getting away from work, and it's just a pleasant thing to do.

And I don't mind landing. It doesn't bother me. I know a lot of people get very nervous, and of course it's much better when it's a well-done landing, but it doesn't bother me.

2

I really don't like checking in. It's very rare that you don't have to stand in a long queue, and that there don't seem to be any complications.

And I really don't like embarking when you haven't got a seat number – going into the airplane and putting up with people pushing around and trying to get to their seat, and not being able to sit with whoever you're travelling with. So, no, I much prefer companies that give you seats.

3

I don't mind going through security if there isn't a long queue, but I hate it when it happens in places like London. Some of the London airports have several hundred people in the queue, and even though they go quite fast, I really dislike that.

I quite like taking off. I've always loved the feeling of leaving the land down there and then just rising in the air suddenly. I really love it.

But I hate the delays. This is something that has happened a lot to me, as well as missing connections, and being in the airport all day. I really hate that.

4

I don't mind waiting to embark. You usually have places to look around, or I take a book and read, and it doesn't bother me too much.

I prefer window seats. I love having a window seat when you can see a new place, some place that you haven't seen before. But if it's a place I've seen before, and it doesn't have anything special in it, I like an aisle seat so I can get up.

I hate waiting for luggage. It's one of the things that often takes too long.

Unit 9 Pronunciation

DDN	DDU	TKT	DAD
DDG	TTT	NTT	
DTD	TGT	DHT	

Unit 9 Listening

Low-cost or traditional?

I=Interviewer, M=Martin Stanton

I Martin, would you mind answering a couple of questions about air travel?

M Of course not. Fire away.

I Could I ask you how often you fly?

M Quite often. Once a month, perhaps. Sometimes twice.

I You travel on College business. Can I ask you if you use low-cost airlines at all?

M I sometimes use them, but I use traditional airlines more.

I Does it bother you to fly with a low-cost carrier?

M No, not especially. Basically, I use what's best for a given trip.

I Which do you prefer – low-cost or traditional?

M In the air there isn't much of a difference. There's more legroom with a traditional airline, perhaps, but that's about all, except, of course, for the chance of business class seats, which are great if you can pay for them. And having your seat number in advance. I hate the race for seats on budget aircraft.

I What about on the ground?

M Well, with traditional airlines you don't need to check in as early. But the biggest difference is when your journey involves two flights. Traditional airlines check your luggage through to your final destination, which is great.

I So, for you cost is the only real advantage of low-cost airlines?

M It's the biggest one, and if you're travelling as a family that's a real advantage. Plus the fact that internet booking seems easier

with budget companies for some reason.
I But would you say that for the business traveller the traditional airlines are still best?
M Yeah, definitely. And I don't see that changing.
I Well, thanks for your time, Martin.
M That's OK. A pleasure.

Unit 10 Listening

At the trade fair

M=Mariana, J=Jurgita

M Wow! That was a tiring day.
J Yes, but wasn't it interesting? I'd quite like to go on most of those trips myself.
M I know what you mean. OK, what have we got?
J Well, in the adventure and action section I thought the water-based activities would be good – diving in the Caribbean, that sort of thing.
M There's also a great trip to Costa Rica: you can combine white-water rafting and biking beneath active volcanoes. You could also do horse riding and stay on a working cattle ranch.
J Sounds good. I think we should recommend a feature on Costa Rica.
M Agreed. What about ecotourism?
J I liked the Antarctica section.
M Me too. There are some fascinating expeditions. There was a great cruise where you get to observe the landscape and the sea-life, and work alongside some of the people down there who are helping to preserve the ecosystem.
J Good. Then we wanted to have a section on 'escape and enlightenment'. There are the regular spa and health resorts of course – there was a good one in Mexico I saw.
M I also liked the pilgrimage to the Seven Holy Cities of India.
J OK, let's go for that – it would be a good contrast to the Costa Rica and Antarctica experiences. Finally, cultural tourism – what did you get?
M Well, it's such a huge range. There are so many possibilities. But the one I liked was the gastronomic week in France staying on a working farm, learning how to cook with natural ingredients, and fitting in with the local life.
J OK, we've got a lot of information and some definite recommendations to give to head office. Did you get all the contact details?
M Yes, I think I managed to …

Unit 10 Listening

Interview with a mountaineer

I=Interviewer, M=Mountaineer

I When did you start mountain climbing?
M I went walking with my parents when I was eight, just in low mountains – hills really. Then I went off with a friend and climbed the same mountains when we were thirteen. I'm surprised our parents let us go, but we got back OK. And we had a great time, so we did it again … and again, and again!
I What about expedition mountaineering? When did you do that?
M That was in 1974. We organized a small expedition. In the end there were two of us. We went to Norway, to the Troll Wall.
I Ah. Do you use a tour company when you organize an expedition, or do you do it yourself?
M For trips in Europe we do it ourselves, and we often do it ourselves in bigger mountains, in fact. I've been to Kenya, Bolivia, Pakistan, Peru – all without a tour company. I've been to Central Asia, too – once to Kyrgyzstan and once to Tajikistan. But both times we used a tour company.
I Why was that?
M Well, it's still quite hard to organize internal transport and permits in these places.
I Hmm. How did you find a suitable company?
M Through the Internet.
I The Internet? So, what do you look for in a tour company? I imagine there's more than one!
M Good question. Well, obviously price is important. That rules out most UK or European companies. Local companies are always cheaper. Then there's the services. You want them to provide the services you need, but without obliging you to take on all the services they offer. We're experienced mountaineers. We don't need a guide from start to finish. Basically, we're looking for a company that will organize local transport up to base camp, base camp food and lodging, permits, and not much else really. So, price, range of services, choice of services, and some indication that they are specialists in mountaineering. Do they use guides who've climbed in the Himalayas? That sort of thing.
I Uh-huh. What's the highest mountain you've climbed?
M One in Tajikistan – a rather pathetic 6,400 metres high. I've been on higher mountains, for example Pic Communism at 7,400 metres high, but I didn't get to the top. But

I've climbed quite a few summits around the 6,000-metre mark. In fact the last one was last month.
I Have you ever been frightened?
M Who hasn't?! Yeah, of course. There isn't a mountaineer who hasn't been scared at some time. If someone says they've never been frightened, they're lying.
I Have you ever thought of giving up?
M Well, I've given up on individual summits – Pic Communism, one in Bolivia, too, and I've had accidents, though I've never had a bad accident. And I've lost friends who've been killed in accidents. That was the worst moment. That hurts for a long time. But I'd never give up mountaineering. I couldn't. Some of my happiest moments have been on big mountains, on the top with friends, or back at base camp enjoying what you did. Fantastic!

Unit 10 Pronunciation

1	vest	3	vine	5	best
2	berry	4	whale	6	veil

Unit 11 Listening

Taking a booking

T =Travel agent, S=Susan Venables

T Hi. Can I help you?
S Yes. We were here last week. We were thinking about a holiday in the Dominican Republic. And you gave us this brochure, and we went away to think.
T Mrs Venables, isn't it?
S Yes, that's right.
T And have you decided on a hotel, or do you need some more help?
S No, we've made our mind up. We thought the Playa Tropical seemed the best for us.
T Mm. Good. A lot of our clients go there. You've made a good choice. So, let me just get a few details down and we can make the booking.
S OK.
T Could you tell me your first name, please?
S Susan.
T OK. And could you give your contact details – your postal address, a daytime telephone number, and an evening number, as well.
S Yes, it's 64 Bridge Lane, Lazenthorpe.
T Is that with a 'z' and a final 'e'?
S That's right – L-A-Z-E-N-T-H-O-R-P-E.
T OK. And a telephone number?
S Er. It's probably easiest to ring my husband on his mobile. That's 0 double 7 479 797 double 9.
T …7 double 9. You don't have an email address, too?

S Yes, it's 'venables.s-r@hotmail.com'.
T …dot 's' hyphen 'r' at hotmail dot com. OK. Now, let's see. Is it just the two of you going?
S That's right.
T And it was for the end of September?
S You've got a good memory! The 21st of September to the 11th of October.
T OK. 21st of the 9th to the 11th of the 10th. And to the Playa Tropical?
S Mm.
T And what about meals? Did you want full board or half board?
S Half board, I think. We want to get out of the hotel and try the local restaurants …
T Which are very good. I'll see if I can find a couple to recommend.
S Oh, that would be nice.
T OK, nearly finished. Let's see if there are any problems. There shouldn't be. No, look, it's come through straight away. Playa Tropical.
S Oh good. That's lovely.
T So if you leave me the deposit, we can confirm the booking.
S How much is it?
T £120 per person. So that's £240 for the two of you.
S And I can pay that by credit card?
T Yes, of course. If you give it to me, I'll just swipe it.
S And when do we pay the rest? I did read it in the conditions …
T You need to pay the balance at least eight weeks before departure. That would be … July twenty seventh. Could you just sign here? So, this is your copy of the booking form. Now, you'll get an invoice through the post within the next two weeks, Mrs Venables. Could you be sure to check the details, and if there were to be any mistakes, let me know, and I'll sort it out for you. OK?
S Lovely. Thanks very much for your help.
T My pleasure. And we're here for anything you need.
S That's great. Bye, then.
T Goodbye.

Unit 11 Listening

The origins of CRSs

I=Interviewer, C=Clemen

I Clemen, could you tell us something about the first computer reservation systems?
C Well, the first system goes back to the 50s, when American Airlines and IBM decided to work together on a computer-based reservation system. The result was known as the Semi-Automatic Business Research Environment, which is quite a mouthful, so

it gets shortened to SABRE.
I Ah, right. SABRE. And is that the same as Amadeus?
C No, no. I mean, they're both computer reservation systems. In that sense they're the same. But they were created by different people at different times. SABRE is an American Airlines creation. That was in 1959. But Amadeus was Air France, Iberia, Scandinavian Airlines, and Lufthansa. And that was quite a lot later.
I Quite a lot later?
C Mm. In 1987.
I So there's SABRE and there's Amadeus. Are there any other systems?
C There's Galileo, and Worldspan, but the two biggest are Amadeus and SABRE. They've each got about about 30% of the market. Galileo's about 25% and Worldspan is much smaller. It's only about 15% of the market. They're all very big, of course. Today we call them GDSs – Global Distribution Systems. Do you know the term GDS?
I Yes. GDSs. And when do Galileo and Worldspan date from?
C Galileo's from 1993. It was a product of British Airways, KLM, Swissair, and Alitalia joining forces.
I Uh-huh. And Worldspan?
C That was in 1990.
I And was that a consortium too?
C Yes. Worldspan was Delta, Northwest Airlines, and TWA – American companies.
I OK, that's interesting. And what about before GDSs …

Unit 11 Pronunciation

finish	same	planned
time	written	change
may	cannot	will
standard	cancel	right
price	pay	higher
if	take	flight
happen	in	

Unit 11 Listening

Handing over tickets

T=Travel agent, B=Mr Bordoni

T Mr Bordoni, nice to see you. You've come for your ticket.
B Yes. Your colleague, Margaret? She rang the office and said I could pick it up. Did you manage to get it any cheaper?
T I'm sorry, Mr Bordoni. We had no luck there.
B I did leave it quite late.
T It was a bit late, but with this fare there's no fee if you need to change the dates of

travel, and it's fully refundable if in the end you can't go.
B Oh well, that's good to know.
T Anyway, here's your ticket, and let's just go through the details. So, that's Toronto–Buenos Aires return, leaving August 12th on flight AC094. Departing Toronto at 23.35 and getting into Buenos Aires the next day at 12.10.
B That's not too bad.
T No, it's a good flight. Then there's your return. That's August 23rd, flight AC093. Depart Buenos Aires at 16.55. Arrive Toronto 06.35. One passenger – yourself. Total costs. Mm, this might hurt. Total cost 3,950 dollars 74 cents.
B Aya! That includes taxes, no?
T That includes taxes, fees, and surcharges.
B And it is refundable?
T One hundred per cent refundable, Mr Bordoni. If you don't go, you don't pay. And as I said, you can change the dates of travel up to two hours before take-off.
B OK. That's good. That's great. Will you bill the company directly?
T No problem.
B Then that's everything, I think.
T Good.
B Thanks for your help.
T Our pleasure, Mr Bordoni.

Unit 12 Listening

An airport worker

I=Interviewer, A=Ali Ghoshal

I Ali, what does your job involve?
A Well, I'm part of the 'turn-around team', as it's called. We're responsible for meeting aircraft when they come in, servicing them, and getting them ready for the outgoing flight.
I How many people work in the team?
A There's about twelve of us. Three technicians like me working on the engines and so on, and then another eight or nine who are responsible for the cabin and in-flight entertainment. My particular responsibility is servicing – putting oil in the engine, checking the technical log for defects reported by the flight crew, that sort of thing.
I What qualifications do you have?
A I studied engineering at university, and I have an Aircraft Maintenance Engineers' licence from the British Civil Aviation Authority.
I Is it a stressful job?
A Yes and no. It's only really the time pressure. We have to get the tasks done in a minimum time.
I What do you like most about your job?
A I suppose the sense of completion. Once

the flight's gone and there are no problems, that's it. And being part of a team and working to a deadline.

I And least?

A The noise pollution, and the dirt and oil and grease. But I can live with that.

I So, you're happy in your job?

A Yes, and I get free air travel which helps.

I Do you have any plans for the future?

A I'm not sure I want to do this forever. I'm taking more engineering qualifications, and I'd like to become a certified engineer eventually.

I Well, good luck, and thanks.

Unit 12 Listening

Two airport dialogues

Conversation A

A Could you help me? I'm trying to find out if a flight has arrived or not.

B Certainly. Are you meeting someone?

A Yes, my brother. He was due in on UA19 from Atlanta. Has it arrived yet?

B Yes, it has. Let me check the status. Here it is. It arrived an hour ago. He should be coming through Gate G about now.

A Right, I'll go there. Gate G, you say?

B Yes, or if he's not at Gate G, try the meeting point.

A That's a good idea. Can you tell me where the meeting point is?

B Yes, of course. It's just over there, next to the newsagent's.

A Thanks for your help.

B You're welcome.

Conversation B

C Hello. Can I have your passport and ticket?

D Here you are.

C Thank you. Are you checking in any bags today?

D Just this one. The other's hand luggage.

C Can you put it on the scales? Thanks. Did you pack it yourself?

D Yes, I did.

C Has anyone interfered with your luggage in any way?

D No, they haven't.

C Are you carrying any sharp objects, such as nail scissors?

D No, I'm not. Erm. Can you tell me if there are any window seats available?

C No, I'm afraid there aren't. The flight's very full. Would you like an aisle seat?

D Yes, that'll do.

C OK. Here's your boarding pass. You'll be boarding through Gate 23 in 30 minutes. Have a nice flight.

D Thank you.

Unit 12 Listening

Two more airport dialogues

Conversation A

A I wonder if you could help me. I was on flight AZ402 and my suitcase hasn't come through yet.

B Flight AZ402? Yes, that should be through by now. Go over to the oversized baggage desk – sometimes bags go there by mistake.

A I've already done that. It's not there. This is very bad, you know. This sort of thing has never happened to me before.

B Yes, I understand. OK, I'll phone through to the baggage people to see if there's anything left below. In the meantime, can you start to fill in this form, so we can trace it? What does the bag look like?

A It's a small brown leather suitcase with a blue ribbon on it. I'm a bit concerned: my sister's meeting me and I know she's going to be getting worried.

B OK, I'll put a message through to the staff in arrivals. What's your sister's name?

A Esther Morgan.

B Thank you. Right. If you just wait over there, we'll sort this out.

Conversation B

C Excuse me, sir. I'm sorry, but you can't go through there.

D Why not? We're going to miss the flight otherwise.

C I'm afraid you're too late – the cabin doors have been shut.

D But I can see the door. Surely they can let us in – we're only five minutes late.

C I'm afraid that's not possible. Once the cabin doors have been shut, no one can go on.

D That's ridiculous! What are we supposed to do? It's your stupid security procedures that made us late in the first place. We're going through anyway. Come on …

C Sir, do not go through the barrier! If you do, I'll have to call security.

D Hmm.

C Thank you, sir. Now, if you see my colleague at the airline desk over there, she'll make sure that you get on the next available flight. You may not have to wait long – there's another flight in an hour or so.

D OK.

Unit 12 Pronunciation

Exercise 1

1 Can you take off your jacket?
2 Can you take off your jacket?
3 I'm sorry, but you can't smoke here.
4 I'm sorry, but you can't smoke here.
5 If you could just take off your jacket.
6 If you could just take off your jacket.
7 I'm afraid this is a no-smoking area.
8 I'm afraid this is a no-smoking area.

Exercise 3

1 Can you take off your jacket?
2 If you could just take off your jacket.
3 I'm sorry, but you can't smoke here.
4 I'm afraid this is a no-smoking area.

Glossary

Vowels

iː	jeep	ʊ	push	aɪ	advice
i	ferry	uː	crew	aʊ	out
ɪ	shift	u	evaluate	ɔɪ	unspoilt
e	seatbelt	ʌ	budget	ɪə	here
æ	bag	ɜː	service	eə	airline
ɑː	market	ə	carrier	ʊə	tour
ɒ	holiday	eɪ	day trip		
ɔː	form	əʊ	code		

Consonants

p	pilot	f	fare	h	hostel
b	baggage	v	visa	m	marina
t	take-off	θ	theme park	n	runway
d	direct	ð	there	ŋ	long-haul
k	cabin	s	sea	l	land
g	gate	z	visit	r	room
tʃ	check-in	ʃ	ship	j	yoga
dʒ	jet	ʒ	leisure	w	waiter

abbreviation /əˌbriːviˈeɪʃn/ *n* a short form of a phrase, word, etc.

advantage /ədˈvɑːntɪdʒ/ *n* a detail that makes a product, for example a holiday, better than similar products

advertise /ˈædvətaɪz/ *v* to tell the public about a product or service in order to encourage people to buy or use it

advice /ədˈvaɪs/ *n* suggestions to somebody about what they could or should do

air conditioning /ˈeə kənˌdɪʃənɪŋ/ *n* a system that cools and dries the air in a building or car **air conditioned** *adj*

air ticket /ˈeə ˌtɪkɪt/ *n* a ticket to travel in a plane

aisle /aɪl/ *n* the passage between rows of seats in a plane

ancient /ˌeɪnʃnt/ adj very old

apartment /əˈpɑːtmənt/ *n* a set of rooms used for holidays

aromatherapy /əˌrəʊməˈθerəpi/ *n* the use of sweet-smelling natural oils to control pain or to encourage relaxation

authentic /ɔːˈθentɪk/ *adj* natural and real; like real life

awareness /əˈweənəs/ *n* the fact of knowing that something, for example a particular company or product, exists

baggage /ˈbægɪdʒ/ *n* personal possessions taken on to a plane by a passenger, including checked luggage and hand luggage

baggage handler /ˈbægɪdʒ ˌhændlə(r)/ *n* a person whose job is to load passengers' luggage on to and off planes

baggage reclaim /ˈbægɪdʒ ˌriːkleɪm/ *n* the place at an airport where you collect your luggage after your flight

balance /ˈbæləns/ *n* an amount of money still owed after some payment has been made

barrier /ˈbæriə(r)/ *n* an object like a fence that stops people from going into a particular area

bed and breakfast /ˌbed ən ˈbrekfəst/ *n* a service that provides a room to sleep in and a meal the next morning in private houses and small hotels

benefit /ˈbenəfɪt/ *n* a helpful and useful effect that something has

boarding pass / boarding card /ˈbɔːdɪŋ pɑːs/ /ˈbɔːdɪŋ kɑːd/ *n* a printed card that airline passengers are given when they check in, that shows their flight and seat number, etc., and that they show before they get on the plane

brochure /ˈbrəʊʃə(r)/ *n* a free magazine that gives information about a company's products and services

browse /braʊz/ *v* to look at different parts of a magazine, the Internet, etc., hoping to find something that interests you

budget /ˈbʌdʒɪt/ *n* 1 the amount of money that you have to spend on something
adj 2 cheap

budget airline /ˌbʌdʒɪt ˈeəlaɪn/ *n* an airline that is cheaper than most airlines, and that usually offers a more basic service

bureau de change /ˌbjʊərəʊ də ˈʃɑːnʒ/ n an office in an airport, etc., where you can exchange foreign currency

business tourism /ˈbɪznəs ˌtʊərɪzm/ n travel that is done for business reasons, for example in order to attend meetings, conferences, and trade fairs

cabin /ˈkæbɪn/ n a small room in a ship or boat, where a passenger sleeps

cabin crew /ˈkæbɪn kruː/ n the people whose job is to take care of passengers on a plane

cable car /ˈkeɪbl kɑː(r)/ n a form of public transport using carriages that are pulled along rails by moving cables

campaign /kæmˈpeɪn/ n a series of planned activities with a particular aim, for example to encourage people to visit a place or to buy something

campsite /ˈkæmpsaɪt/ n a place where people on holiday can put up their tents, park their caravan, camper, etc., often with toilets, water, etc.

cancel /ˈkænsl/ v to decide that you no longer want to do what you have arranged to do, for example go on a holiday

cancellation /ˌkænsəˈleɪʃn/ n a decision that you no longer want to do what you have arranged to do, for example go on a holiday

carnival /ˈkɑːnɪvl/ n a public festival with lively music and dancing in the streets

carriage /ˈkærɪdʒ/ n a separate section of a train, tram, or similar form of public transport

carrier code /ˈkærɪə kəʊd/ n a series of numbers that identify a particular airline

catering /ˈkeɪtərɪŋ/ n the work of providing food and drinks for people

cathedral /kəˈθiːdrəl/ n a large church that is the most important one in a city

cattle ranch /ˈkætl rɑːntʃ/ n a very large farm, especially in the US or Australia, where cows are kept

charter flight /ˈtʃɑːtə flaɪt/ n a flight which a travel company pays for and then sells seats to its customers, especially as part of a package holiday

check-in clerk /ˈtʃek ɪn klɑːk/ n a person who works for an airline, who checks passengers' tickets and passports when they arrive at the airport, takes their luggage, and gives them a boarding card

chef /ʃef/ n a person whose job is to cook food in a restaurant, hotel, etc.

client /ˈklaɪənt/ n a person who uses the services of a company

climate /ˈklaɪmɪt/ n the normal pattern of weather conditions in a particular place

coastline /ˈkəʊstlaɪn/ n the land along a coast, next to the sea

commission /kəˈmɪʃn/ n an amount of money that is paid to somebody for selling something, that increases with the amount they sell

concrete /ˈkɒnkriːt/ n a hard, grey building material

conductor /kənˈdʌktə(r)/ n a person whose job is collect passengers' fares on a bus, train, etc.

conference /ˈkɒnfərəns/ n a large official meeting, often lasting several days, for members of an organization or company to discuss subjects related to their work

conference facilities /ˈkɒnfərəns fəˌsɪlətiz/ n the rooms, equipment, services, etc. that are necessary for holding a conference

confirm /kənˈfɜːm/ v to check or to announce that something will definitely happen as originally planned

connecting flight /kəˌnektɪŋ ˈflaɪt/ n a segment of a flight that requires a passenger to change planes, but not change carriers

conservation /ˌkɒnsəˈveɪʃn/ n the protection of the natural environment

contact details /ˈkɒntækt ˈdiːteɪlz/ n your email address and phone number, and possibly your home address, fax number, etc.

convince /kənˈvɪns/ v to make somebody believe something so that they feel confident

cottage /ˈkɒtɪdʒ/ n a small house, especially in the country

country house /ˌkʌntri ˈhaʊs/ n a large, expensive house in the country

countryside /ˈkʌntrisaɪd/ n land outside towns and cities, with fields, woods, etc.

CRS, computerized reservation system /ˌsiː ɑːr ˈes/ /kəmˌpjuːtəraɪzd rezəˈveɪʃn ˌsɪstəm/ n a system for booking a hotel room, a flight, etc. on the Internet

cruise ship /ˈkruːz ʃɪp/ n a large boat that carries passengers to different places as part of a holiday

customs /ˈkʌstəmz/ n the place at an airport where your bags are checked as you come into a country

day trip /ˈdeɪ trɪp/ n a tour or excursion that leaves in the morning and returns the same evening

delay /dɪˈleɪz/ n a period of time where you have to wait

departure gate /dɪˈpɑːtʃə geɪt/ n a numbered area in an airport where passengers get on their plane

departure lounge /dɪˈpɑːtʃə laʊndʒ/ n an area in an airport where passengers wait before getting on their plane

deposit details /dɪˈpɒzɪt ˌdiːteɪlz/ n a record of the amount of money that a customer has paid as the first part of a larger payment

desert /ˈdezət/ n a large area of land that has very little water and very few plants growing on it

destination /ˌdestɪˈneɪʃn/ n a place that people travel to, for example on holiday

develop /dɪˈveləp/ v to think of a new product and work on it so that it will be successful

direct dial telephone /daɪˌrekt ˈdaɪl/ *n* a telephone that allows you to call somebody directly without having to speak to reception or a switchboard first

direct flight /daɪˌrekt ˈflaɪt/ *n* a flight that does not involve changing planes

direct selling /daɪˌrekt ˈselɪŋ/ *n* the practice of selling products and services directly to the public, without using shops, agents, etc.

diving /ˈdaɪvɪŋ/ *n* the activity of swimming under the surface of the sea, a lake, etc.

domestic /dəˈmestɪk/ *adj* operating inside its own country

domestic tourism /dəˌmestɪk ˈtʊərɪzəm/ *n* the activity of people taking holidays in their own country

ecotourism /ˌiːkəʊ ˈtʊərɪzm/ *n* tourism designed so that the tourists damage the environment as little as possible, especially when some of the money they pay is used to protect the local environment and animals

emissions /ɪˈmɪʃənz/ *n* gases that are sent out into the air

enlightenment /ɪnˈlaɪtənmnt/ *n* a deeper understanding of life, especially of feelings and beliefs outside the physical world

enormous /ɪˈnɔːməs/ *adj* very big

en-suite (facilities) /ˌɒn swiːt fəˈsɪlətɪz/ *adj* (of a bedroom) having a private bathroom joined on

escalator /ˈeskəleɪtə(r)/ *n* moving stairs that carry people between different floors of a large building

establish /ɪˈstæblɪʃ/ *v* to form or create something for the first time

evaluate /ɪˈvæljueɪt/ *v* to make a judgement, for example about how successful something is, after thinking about it carefully

excursion /ɪksˈkɜːʃn/ *n* a short journey for pleasure that is organized for a group of people

expectation /ˌekspkˈteɪʃn/ *n* a belief about what something will or should be like, for example a product

expedition /ˌekspəˈdɪʃn/ *n* an organized journey to a place that not many people go to because it is difficult to get to

expenditure /ɪksˈpendɪtʃə(r)/ *n* the amount of money that a person or company spends

fam trip, familiarization trip /ˈfæm trɪp/ /fəˌmɪljəraɪˈzeɪʃn trɪp/ *n* a visit organized by an airline or tourist resort, etc., where tour operators and journalists can get to know the facilities and services offered

fare /feə(r)/ *n* the money that you pay to travel by plane, train, taxi, etc.

feature /ˈfiːtʃə(r)/ *n* one of the details that describes a particular product or service

ferry /ˈferi/ *n* a boat that carries passengers between two points of land, between two islands, etc.

five-star /ˌfaɪv ˈstɑː(r)/ *adj* (used about a hotel) of the highest quality

flight attendant /ˈflaɪt əˌtendənt/ *n* a person whose job is to serve and take care of passengers on a plane

fly-drive holiday /ˌflaɪ draɪv ˈhɒlɪdeɪ/ *n* a package that includes the cost of both the flight and hire of a car at the destination

foreign currency /ˌfɒrən ˈkʌrənsi/ *n* the notes and coins that are used as money in another country

gastronomic /ˌgæstrəˈnɒmɪk/ *adj* connected with cooking and eating good food

GDS, global distribution system /ˌdʒiː diː ˈes/ /ˌgləʊbl dɪstrɪˈbjuːʃn ˌsɪstəm/ *n* a very large system that allows you to book hotels, flights, etc. in different parts of the world on the Internet

ground crew /ˈgraʊnd kruː/ *n* the people at an airport whose job is to take care of planes while they are on the ground

guarantee /ˌgærənˈtiː/ *v* to make a firm, official promise that something will (or will not) happen

guard /gɑːd/ *n* a person who is in charge of a train and travels with it, but does not drive it

guest house /ˈgest haʊs/ *n* a small hotel, usually run by the person or family that owns it

harbour /ˈhɑːbə(r)/ *n* a place on the coast where ships can be tied up, that is protected from the sea and bad weather

health farm /ˈhelθ fɑːm/ *n* a place where you can stay for a short period of time in order to try to improve your health by eating special food, doing physical exercise, etc.

heritage /ˈherɪtɪdʒ/ *n* the traditions, culture, and history of a place

high-rise /ˈhaɪ raɪz/ *adj* (of a building) very tall, with many floors

hillwalking /ˈhɪl ˌwɔːkɪŋ/ *n* the activity of going for long walks in the hills for pleasure

historic monument /hɪˌstɒrɪk ˈmɒnjumənt/ *n* a famous building, column, statue, etc. that has special historical importance

hostel /ˈhɒstəl/ *n* a building that provides cheap accommodation, often in rooms with several beds, and meals for travellers

hovercraft /ˈhɒvəkrɑːft/ *n* a vehicle that travels just above the surface of water or land, held up by air being forced downwards

identify /aɪˈdentɪfaɪ/ *v* to find out or discover what something is

immigration /ˌɪmɪˈgreɪʃn/ *n* the place at an airport where the passports and other documents of people coming into a country are checked

improve /ɪmˈpruːv/ *v* to make something better

in advance /ˌɪn ədˈvɑːns/ *adv* before the time when something will happen, be used, etc.

in bulk /ɪn ˈbʌlk/ *adv* in large quantities, and usually at a reduced price

inbound tourism /ˌɪnbaʊnd ˈtʊərɪzm/ *n* the activity of people entering the country from abroad to take holidays

incentive tour /ɪnˈsentɪv ˌtʊə(r)/ *n* a journey or holiday given to a worker or group of workers as a reward for good work

include /ɪnˈkluːd/ *v* to have something as one part

inclusive tour /ɪnˌkluːsɪv ˈtʊə(r)/ *n* a holiday that includes transport, accommodation, and sometimes other things such as meals and excursions

incoming /ˈɪnkʌmɪŋ/ *adj* connected with travel into the country from abroad

independent /ˌɪndɪˈpendənt/ *adj* 1. (used about a traveller) making their own arrangements for travel, rather than going on a package holiday *adj* 2. (used about a country) having its own government

initial enquiry form /ɪˌnɪʃl ɪnˈkwaɪri fɔːm/ *n* a form on which a company records details about the type of product or service a new customer is looking for, and the customer's contact details

innovative /ˈɪnəvətɪv/ *adj* new and interesting

insurance /ɪnˈʃʊərəns/ *n* an arrangement with a company where you pay them a small amount of money before you travel, and they agree to pay the costs if you are ill or die, or lose or damage something

inventory /ˈɪnvəntri/ *n* details of a flight booking, including flight number, time, route, seat number, etc.

investigate /ɪnˈvestɪɡeɪt/ *v* to find out information, for example by asking somebody a number of questions

issue /ˈɪʃuː/ *v* to give somebody something official, for example a ticket, passport, etc.

itinerary /aɪˈtɪnərəri/ *n* a list of things that will happen, for example on a tour, and their times

jeep /dʒiːp/ *n* a small strong vehicle used especially for driving over rough ground

key data /ˌkiː ˈdeɪtə/ *n* the most important information

land /lænd/ *v* (used about a plane) to arrive at an airport

landscape /ˈlændskeɪp/ *n* everything you can see when you look across a large area of land, especially in the country

leisure tourism /ˈleʒə ˌtʊərɪzm/ *n* travel that is done just for pleasure, rather than for business or for a specific purpose

long-haul /ˌlɒŋ ˈhɔːl/ *adj* (of a flight) covering a long distance

lost property /ˌlɒst ˈprɒpəti/ *n* the place at an airport, etc. where items that have been found are kept until they are collected

low-cost carrier /ˌləʊ kɒst ˈkæriə/ *n* an airline that is cheaper than most airlines, and that usually offers a more basic service

luxury /ˈlʌkʃəri/ *adj* very comfortable and high quality

marina /məˈriːnə/ *n* a specially designed harbour for private boats

market /ˈmɑːkɪt/ *v* to show and advertise a product to the public

marketing /ˈmɑːkɪtɪŋ/ *n* the activity of showing and advertising a company's products in the best possible way

massage /ˈmæsɑːʒ/ *n* the activity of having your body rubbed, pressed, etc. in order to help you relax

maximum stay /ˌmæksɪməm ˈsteɪ/ *n* the longest possible time between travelling to a place and travelling back

meal basis /ˈmiːl ˌbeɪsɪs/ *n* an agreement of how many meals will be provided as part of a holiday package, for example bed and breakfast or full board

mechanic /məˈkænɪk/ *n* a person whose job is to make sure that a plane's engines are working correctly, and to repair them if necessary

meditation /ˌmedɪˈteɪʃn/ *n* the activity of thinking deeply in a quiet place, in order to make your mind calm

meeting room /ˈmiːtɪŋ rʊm/ *n* a room designed for business meetings to be held in

metropolitan /ˌmetrəˈpɒlɪtən/ *adj* in or connected with a large or capital city

minimum stay /ˌmɪnɪməm ˈsteɪ/ *n* the shortest possible time between travelling to a place and travelling back

monitor /ˈmɒnɪtə(r)/ *v* to watch and check something over a period of time

motivation /ˌməʊtɪˈveɪʃn/ *n* something that makes you want to do a particular thing, for example travel to a particular place

motorway (AmE = freeway) /ˈməʊtəweɪ/ *n* a wide road, usually with three or more lanes in each direction, where traffic can travel fast for long distances between large towns

mountain climbing /ˈmaʊntɪn ˌklaɪmɪŋ/ *n* the activity of climbing mountains as a sport

mountaineer /ˌmaʊntɪˈnɪə(r)/ *n* a person who climbs mountains as a sport

non-stop flight /ˌnɒn stɒp ˈflaɪt/ *n* a flight without any stops

online /ˈɒnlaɪn/ *adj* operating on the Internet

open-jaw trip /ˌəʊpən ˈdʒɔː trɪp/ *n* a return air ticket that allows you to fly into a country at one airport, and leave the country by a different airport

operator /ˈɒpəreɪtə(r)/ *n* a company that provides travel services

opportunity /ˌɒpəˈtjuːnəti/ *n* something that gives you the chance to be successful

outbound tourism /ˌaʊtbaʊnd ˈtʊərɪzm/ *n* the activity of people leaving their country to take holidays

overnight /ˌəʊvəˈnaɪt/ *v* to stay for one night

package holiday / tour /ˌpækɪdʒ ˈhɒlɪdeɪ/ˌtʊə(r)/ *n* a holiday that includes transport, accommodation, and sometimes other things such as meals and excursions

paperless ticketing /ˌpeɪpələs ˈtɪkɪtɪŋ/ n a system where passengers book air tickets on the Internet or over the phone. No ticket is necessary as the information is stored on the airline's computers.

passenger flow /ˈpæsɪndʒə fləʊ/ n the number of passengers coming into and going out of an airport

passport control /ˌpɑːspɔːt kənˈtrəʊl/ n a place in an airport where you have to show your passport to an official as you pass through

picturesque /ˌpɪktʃəˈresk/ adj (of a place) pretty and old-fashioned

pier /ˈpɪə(r)/ n a long, low structure built in the sea and joined to the land at one end

pilgrimage /ˈpɪlgrɪmɪdʒ/ n a journey to an important religious place

pilot /ˈpaɪlət/ n a person whose job is to fly planes

porter /ˈpɔːtə(r)/ n 1 a person whose job is carrying people's bags and other loads, especially at a train station, an airport, or in a hotel 2 a person whose job is to be in charge of the entrance to a hotel

present /prɪˈzent/ v to show something, for example a new product, to people for the first time, and tell them about it

product /ˈprɒdʌkt/ n something that a company sells

promotional /prəˈməʊʃənl/ adj used, done, etc. in order to advertise something

provider /prəˈvaɪdə(r)/ n a company that provides a particular service, for example an airline or a hotel group

public sector /ˌpʌblɪk ˈsektə(r)/ n the part of the economy of a country that is owned or controlled by the government

purser /ˈpɜːsə(r)/ n an officer on a ship who is responsible for taking care of the passengers, and for the accounts

raise /reɪz/ v to increase something

rapport /ræˈpɔː(r)/ n a friendly and understanding relationship between two people

receipt /rɪˈsiːt/ n a piece of paper that is given to show that you have paid for something

receptionist /rɪˈsepʃənɪst/ n a person whose job is to deal with people arriving at or telephoning a hotel

refuge /ˈrefjuːdʒ/ n a very simple building that provides shelter and protection from the weather

remote /rɪˈməʊt/ adj (of a place) far away from other places where people live

rep, representative /rep/ ˌreprəˈzentətɪv/ n a person whose job is to look after people who are on a package holiday

requirement /rɪˈkwaɪəmnt/ n something that a person needs

research /rɪˈsɜːtʃ/ v to make a careful study of something in order to find out information

resort rep /rɪˈzɔːt rep/ n = rep

retail /ˈriːteɪl/ n the business of selling things, for example holidays and tours, to the public

retreat /rɪˈtriːt/ n a quiet, private place that you go to in order to get away from your usual life

retrieve data /rɪˌtriːv ˈdeɪtə/ v to find and look at information that has been stored on a computer

return trip /rɪˌtɜːn ˈtrɪp/ n an air journey that departs from and arrives back at the same airport

room service /ˈrʊm ˌsɜːvɪs/ n a service provided in a hotel, where guests can order food and drink to be brought to their rooms

runway /ˈrʌnweɪ/ n a long narrow strip of ground in an airport, that planes take off from and land on

safari /səˈfɑːri/ n a trip to see wild animals, especially in Africa

sales consultant /ˈseɪlz kənˌsʌltnt/ n a person whose job is to give customers information and advice in order to help them buy the product that is right for them

sales process /ˈseɪlz ˌprəʊses/ n all the activities that happen between a

customer first knowing that a product exists, and buying the product

scales /skeɪlz/ n a machine for weighing things, for example bags at an airport

scheduled airline /ˌskedjuːld ˈeəlaɪn/ n an airline that operates to fixed timetables and on fixed routes, and which sells tickets to the public rather than to package holiday companies

sea view /ˌsiː ˈvjuː/ n the possibility to see the sea from the window

seatbelt /ˈsiːtbelt/ n a belt that is attached to the seat in a plane and that you fasten around yourself

secondary airport /ˌsekəndri ˈeəpɔːt/ n a small airport that is not one of the main ones in a country

security check /sɪˈkjʊərəti tʃek/ n the process of checking passengers and their bags at an airport to make sure that they are not carrying anything dangerous

security control /sɪˈkjʊərəti kənˌtrəʊl/ n the place in an airport where passengers and their bags go through a metal detector to make sure they are not carrying dangerous objects

self-catering /ˌself ˈkeɪtərɪŋ/ adj (of holiday accommodation) in which you provide your own meals

service station /ˈsɜːvɪs ˌsteɪʃn/ n an area and building beside a motorway where you can buy food and petrol, go to the toilet, etc.

serviced /ˈsɜːvɪst/ adj (of holiday accommodation) in which meals are provided

shift /ʃɪft/ n one of the working periods that a 24-hour day is divided into. When a shift ends, one group of workers stops and another group begins.

short-haul /ˈʃɔːt hɔːl/ adj (of a flight) covering a short distance

shuttle /ˈʃʌtl/ n a plane, bus, or train that travels regularly between two places

skilled /skɪld/ *adj* (of a job) that requires special ability or training

spa /spɑː/ *n* a place where people can relax and improve their health, often where hot water comes naturally to the surface from under the ground

specialist /ˈspeʃəlɪst/ *adj* dealing with one kind of thing only; not general

spectacular /spekˈtækjələ(r)/ *adj* very impressive to see

steward /ˈstjuːəd/ *n* a man whose job is to take care of passengers on a ship, a plane, or a train and who brings them meals, etc.

stopover /ˈstɒpəʊvə(r)/ *n* an interruption to a trip lasting twelve or more hours

store data /stɔː ˈdeɪtə/ *v* to keep information on a computer until you need to use it

strength /streŋθ/ *n* a good quality that you have that gives you an advantage

study tour /ˈstʌdi tʊə(r)/ *n* a trip to a country or an area that includes visits, lectures, and classes

suite /swiːt/ *n* a set of rooms in a hotel

supplement /ˈsʌplɪmnt/ *n* an extra amount of money that you have to pay for an additional service or item

surcharge /ˈsɜːtʃɑːdʒ/ *n* an extra amount of money that you have to pay in addition to the usual price

t'ai chi /ˌtaɪ ˈtʃiː/ *n* a Chinese system of physical exercises designed especially to make your mind calm

take-off /ˈteɪk ɒf/ *n* the process of a plane leaving an airport

tariff /ˈtærɪf/ *n* the fixed price for a service

tax /tæks/ *n* an amount of money from your income that you have to pay to the government

temperate /ˈtempərət/ *adj* (of a place's climate) not very hot and not very cold

temple /ˈtempl/ *n* a building where people of some religions, for example Hindus and Buddhists, go to pray

terminal /ˈtɜːmɪnl/ *n* the airport building that has all the facilities for passengers that are arriving or departing

terminus /ˈtɜːmɪnəs/ *n* the last station at the end of a railway line or the last stop on a bus route

theme park /ˈθiːm pɑːk/ *n* a large park with rides, such as roller-coasters, and many other kinds of entertainment

threat /θret/ *n* something that could stop you being successful, for example a strong competitor

ticket collector /ˈtɪkɪt kəˌlektə(r)/ *n* a person whose job is to check passengers' tickets for travelling on a train, boat, etc.

tiny /ˈtaɪni/ *adj* very small

tour guide /ˈtʊə gaɪd/ *n* a person whose job is to show tourists around places

tour operator /ˈtʊə ˌɒpəreɪtə(r)/ *n* a person or company that organizes and sells package holidays

tourist attraction /ˈtʊərɪst əˌtrækʃn/ *n* a place that tourists visit

tourist flow /ˈtʊərɪst fləʊ/ *n* the movement of people into, out of, and inside a country, when they are on holiday

tourist information officer /ˌtʊərɪst ɪnfəˈmeɪʃn ˌɒfɪsə(r)/ *n* a person whose job is to give advice and help to tourists who are visiting a city, town, etc.

track /træk/ *n* metal rails that trains, trams, etc. travel along

trade fair /ˈtreɪd feə(r)/ *n* a large exhibition and meeting for advertising and selling products

transfer /ˈtrænsfɜː(r)/ *n* 1 travel to and from the airport and your hotel *v* 2 to travel to or from the airport and your hotel

travel agent /ˈtrævl ˌeɪdʒnt/ *n* a person or company whose business is to make travel arrangements for people, for example buying tickets, arranging hotel rooms, or selling package holidays

travel insurance /ˈtrævl ɪnˌʃʊərəns/ *n* an arrangement with a company where you pay them a small amount of money before you travel, and they agree to pay the costs if you are ill or die, or lose or damage something

trek /trek/ *n* a long hard walk lasting several days or weeks, usually in the mountains

trend /trend/ *n* a general direction in which something is increasing or decreasing

trolley /ˈtrɒli/ *n* a small vehicle with wheels that you carry your luggage on and push around at an airport

turnaround time /ˈtɜːnəraʊnd ˌtaɪm/ *n* the time between a plane landing at an airport and taking off again

unspoilt /ʌnˈspɔɪlt/ *adj* (of a place) beautiful because it has not been changed or built on

VFR, visiting friends and relatives /ˌviː ef ˈɑː(r)/ /ˌvɪzɪtɪŋ ˌfrendz ənd ˈrelətɪvz/ *n* travel that is done in order to visit friends or family

visa /ˈviːzə/ *n* an official mark or piece of paper that shows you are allowed to enter, leave, or travel through a particular country

volcano /vɒlˈkeɪnəʊ/ *n* a mountain with a large opening at the top through which gases and hot, liquid rock sometimes come out

waiter /ˈweɪtə(r)/ *n* a person whose job is to take food orders and serve food in a restaurant, bar, etc.

wake-up call /ˈweɪk ʌp ˌkɔːl/ *n* a telephone call that you arrange to be made to you in a hotel, in order to wake you up

weakness /ˈwiːknəs/ *n* a quality you have that makes it more difficult for you to be successful

wedding /ˈwedɪŋ/ *n* a ceremony where two people get married

weekend break /ˌwiːkend ˈbreɪk/ *n* a trip, often to a city or countryside hotel, that includes Saturday and Sunday

whale-watching /ˈweɪl ˌwɒtʃɪŋ/ *n* going on a boat trip to see whales swimming in the sea

white-water rafting /ˌwaɪt wɔːtə ˈrɑːftɪŋ/ *n* the activity of travelling down a fast-flowing river in a rubber boat

wholesaler /ˈhəʊlseɪlə(r)/ *n* a company that sells goods or services in large quantities to other companies, which sell them to the public

wildlife /ˈwaɪldlaɪf/ *n* animals, birds, etc. that are wild and live in a natural environment

windsurfing /ˈwɪndsɜːfɪŋ/ *n* the sport of sailing on water standing on a long narrow board with a sail

worldwide /ˌwɜːldˈwaɪd/ *adj* in all parts of the world

yacht /jɒt/ *n* a large sailing boat, often also with an engine and a place to sleep on board, used for pleasure trips and racing

yoga /ˈjəʊɡə/ *n* a system of exercises and breathing that helps you control and relax your mind and body

Great Clarendon Street, Oxford OX2 6DP

Oxford University Press is a department of the University of Oxford.
It furthers the University's objective of excellence in research, scholarship,
and education by publishing worldwide in

Oxford New York

Auckland Cape Town Dar es Salaam Hong Kong Karachi
Kuala Lumpur Madrid Melbourne Mexico City Nairobi
New Delhi Shanghai Taipei Toronto

With offices in

Argentina Austria Brazil Chile Czech Republic France Greece
Guatemala Hungary Italy Japan Poland Portugal Singapore
South Korea Switzerland Thailand Turkey Ukraine Vietnam

OXFORD and OXFORD ENGLISH are registered trade marks of
Oxford University Press in the UK and in certain other countries

© Oxford University Press 2006

ACKNOWLEDGEMENTS

*The authors and publisher are grateful to those who have given permission to reproduce
the following extracts and adaptations of copyright material:*

p.24 adapted extracts from *A Glimpse of the Baltics Tour* from the Scantours
website. Used by kind permission of www.scantours.com

p.33 adapted extract from *Getting off the beaten track* by R Foroohar from
Newsweek (22/29 July 2002) © Newsweek Inc. All rights reserved. Reprinted
by permission.

p.33 adapted extract from *The State of Tourism* by Melvyn Pryer. Used by kind
permission of the author.

p.42 adapted extracts from *Travel agent myths and realities* from the American
Society of Travel Agents website. Used by kind permission of
www.astanet.com

p.53 adapted extracts from *Summer Jobs Britain 2005.* Used by kind permission
of Vacation Work Publications.

p.64 adapted extracts from the accommodation section of the Visit Scotland
website. Used by kind permission of www.visitscotland.com

p.65 adapted extracts from the Unusual Hotels of the World website. Used by
kind permission of www.unusualhotelsoftheworld.com © 2006.

p.70 adapted extracts from *The Tourists' Top Ten* from the NewcastleGateshead
Initiative website. Used by kind permission of www.NewcastleGateshead.com

p.85 adapted extracts from *The Karakoram Experience* on the KE Adventure
Travel website. Used by kind permission of www.keadventure.com

p.88 adapted extracts from *Tourism in Antarctica* from the Cool Antarctica
website. Used by kind permission of www.coolantarctica.com

p.104 adapted extracts from *Air Passenger Rights* from the EU website. Used by
kind permission of http://europa.eu.net © European Communities 1995–2006.

p.116 adapted extracts from The Pilgrimage Route of St James 2006 from the
World Walks website. Used by kind permission of www.worldwalks.com

Sources:

p.46 *Tourism: Principles, Practices, Philosophies* by Charles R Goedner
& J.R. Brent Ritchie.
p.78 www.iata.org
p.94 www.wikipedia.org

*The authors and publisher are grateful to the following for their permission to reproduce
photographs and illustrative material:*

Alamy Images pp.10 (poster / Mary Evans Picture Library), 12 (beach
/Bowmann / f1 online), 16 (geyser / Jon Arnold Images), 18 (club / Debbie
Bragg / Everynight Images), 20 (tour guide / Images&Stories), 23 (trade show /
Steven May), 26 (coaches / CaptialCity Images), 30 (airport lounge / Russ
Merne), 33 (Gran Canaria hotel / James Davis), 38 (Uluru-Ayers Rock /
nagelstock.com), 47 (San Francisco / Richard Wareham Fotografie), 60 (Joe
Sohm / Visions of America, LLC), 70 (Gateshead bridge / Paul Thompson
Images), 74 (Hong Kong / Stock Connection Distribution), 84 (white-water
rafting / StockShot), 97 (credit cards / Peter Bowater), 103 (airport lounge / R.
Henning / Archiverlin Fotoagentur GmbH), 118 (Loch Voil Scotland / John
Prior Images); BAA Aviation Picture Library pp.81 (aircraft fins), 102
(information desk); Ballymaloe House p.61; Corbis pp.4 (reception / M.
Thomsen / zefa), 12 (Neuschwanstein Castle / Hubert Spichtinger / zefa), 31
(Mecca / Kazuyoshi Nomachi), 32 (leopard / Joe McDonald), 46 (Cadillac /
Martyn Goddard), 49 (Amtrak train / Millepost 92 1/2), 60 (log cabin / Peter
Beck), 64 (Isle of Skye / Dridmar Damm / Zefa), 67 (receptionist / Denis Cooper
/ zefa), 73 (Kyrgistan / Buddy Mays), 74 (grapes / Owen Franken), 84 (orca /
Stuart Westmorland), 85 (trekkers), 88 (cruise ship / Paul A. Sounders), 98
(businesswoman / Michael Prince), 100 (airport / Jim Richardson); El Hana
Hotels p.61; Gamirasu Hotel p.65; Getty Images cover (Deborah Jaffe / Taxi);
pp.4 (guide / Kelvin Murray / Stone), 10 (Skegness diver / Felix Man / Hulton
Archive), 12 (Sicily / Kefin Schafer / Stone), 14 (Hawaii/ Lisa Beardon / Stone+),
16 (bunjee / Anne-Marie Weber / Taxi), 24 (Vilnius / Peter Adams / Image
Bank), 32 (Mount Kenya / Bobby Model / National Geographic), 39 (Sydney
harbour / Peter Hendrie / Image Bank), 40 (young woman / Dirk Anschutz /
Taxi), 42 (beach scene / Ed Freeman / Image Bank), 52 (young woman / Hans
Carlem / Johner Images), 60 (camping site / KitStock / Photonica), 63 (woman
in the mountains / Jochem D. Wijnands / Image Bank), 67 (man on the phone
/ Robert Warren / Stone), 71 (Warkworth Castle / Joe Cornish / DK Images), 73
(beach in Croatia / Peter Higgins / Robert Harding World Imagery), 80
(businessman / Jakob Helbig Photography / Photonica), 85 (mountain biking /
Andrew O'Toole / Photonica), 86 (mountaineer / David Trood / Stone+), 88
(penguins / Theo Allofs / Stone+), 89 (ger / Peter Adams / Image Bank); Lonely
Planet Images p.73 (fjord in Sweden / Anders Blomqvist); LumiLinna p.65
(snow hotel); Magnum Photos pp.10 (tourist on a pony / Martin Parr), 116
(pilgrim / Jean Gaumy); News Team International p.36 (BA shop / Shaun
Fellows); OUP pp.6 (tropical beach / Photodisc), 7 (woman / Image Source), 20
(family on beach / Photodisc); Photolibrary.com pp.16 (Queenstown, New
Zealand / Chris McLennan), 18 (Sagrada Familia / Japack Photo Library), 25
(Tallin old town / Jon Arnold Images), 112 (spa pool / Tim Street-Porter / Beate
Works Inc.); Punchstock pp.4 (pilot / Digital Vision), 8 (man with glasses /
Photodisc), 18 (Scottish landscape / Corbis), 20 (young woman / Corbis), 36
(travel agent / ImageSource), 93 (couple with travel agent / KomStock
Images), 102 (customs officer / Digital Vision); Radisson SAS p.61; Rex
Features p.36 (Going Places shop); Tips Images p.56 (Lucia Invernizzi Tettoni);
Superstock pp.12 (Disney World / Steve Vidler), 18 (Prague / age fotostock), 22
(Burma / age footstock), 32 (beach, Kenya / age footstock), 70 (Angel of the
North / Brian Lawrence), 98 (Shanghai / age footstock); The Flight Collection
p.102 (check-in / Loasby).

Illustrations by:

AIGA p.101; Pierre d'Alancaisez pp.98, 99; David Atkinson / NB Illustration
pp.12, 16, 22, 24, 32, 41, 44, 79, 88; Mark Duffin p.66; Roger Full / Industrial
Art Studio pp.50, 100; Dylan Gibson pp.9, 15, 26, 35, 39, 47, 66, 69, 82, 91, 95,
106 (Customer care); Tim Kahane pp.8, 14, 21, 29, 34, 37, 60, 62, 68 (flow
diagram), 72, 77, 104, 106 (signs); Stephanie Wunderlich / Three in a Box
pp.28, 68 (advert), 76, 84, 87, 90, 92, 96.

*The authors and publisher would like to thank the many teachers, schools, and
institutions who assisted in the development of this title, in particular:*

Celina Alvarez Valle, *Camping Picos de Europa,* Asturias, Spain; *Jenny Brown
Travel,* Madrid, Spain; Javier Diez, *Aeropostal,* Caracas, Venezuela; Elmira
Haibullina, *Tourasia,* Almaty, Kazakhstan; Karen Marshall, *NewcastleGateshead
Initiative,* Tyne and Wear, UK; Begoña Moran, *Berkana Travel Tours,* Rio de
Janeiro, Brazil; John Muhoho, *CKC Tours and Travel,* Nairobi, Kenya; Begoña
Pozo, *Myanmar Gold,* Vigo, Spain; Clemen Rodríguez, *Escuela Universitaria de
Turismo de Asturias,* Oviedo, Spain; Martin Stanton & Melvyn Prior, *Birmingham
College of Food, Tourism and Creative Studies,* Birmingham, UK; Andrew Sharpe,
Authentic Caribbean Holidays Ltd, Kingston, Jamaica; *Viajes Tebas,* Oviedo, Spain.